MURPHY'S WILL

MURPHY'S WILL

EDWARD A. McCOYD

NEW STREET
PUBLISHING

To Donna and the Vermont we loved

— 1 —

MIKE HEARD IT FIRST. There was a strange noise coming from the office next door, the one Mike and his partner had rented to a solo practitioner named Max Karraten. It sounded like a woman on the verge of hysteria, calling his name—"Max, Max, what's the matter, Max. Someone, anyone, help! Help!"

Mike jumped up from his desk and ran into the hallway outside their office. The cries were getting louder. "Max, are you all right? Max, you're not breathing! Help! Is anyone out there?" Her voice was coming from Karraten's office, but the door was locked. Mike pounded on it.

Mike could hear high heels clicking on the floor on the other side of the door. Then the door opened, and a middle-aged woman, her face flushed and streaked with tears, stood before him.

"He's on the floor in his office. He started choking and tried to get up, and then he fell over onto the floor. He won't wake up. I don't think he's breathing. Do something, please."

She sobbed and moved out of the way so Mike could pass. He went toward the open door to Karraten's private office, where the older attorney lay on his back, motionless.

Entering, Mike knelt by the man's side. He bent his tall frame over the apparently lifeless body, and leaned in to see if he could detect any breathing.

"What's the matter, Mike?"

Mike looked up.

The words came from Mike's partner, Tim, who had followed after him when he heard the commotion.

"It looks bad, Tim. Call 911. I'll try CPR."

Mike used both hands to repeatedly press down on the man's chest, but without effect, as Tim grabbed the phone and dialed 911. The woman, horrified, continued to sob.

Less than ten minutes later, an emergency crew rushed into the room and took over for Mike, but after only a few more minutes they stopped and looked up.

"He's gone."

AFTER THE EMS CREW and the responding policemen left with the body, the lady sank into a chair and moaned.

"How will I pay the rent now? I needed that money."

"What money, miss?" asked Mike.

"From the car accident. Max had the settlement check for me, but it's made out to both of us. I came in to sign it so he could deposit it in his escrow account. He said that once it cleared, he'd take his fee and give me the rest. That's the check, there on his desk." She pointed.

Mike reached for the check and turned it over. The name Madeline Murphy was neatly written on the back. There was no other signature. Max Karraten obviously knew better than to sign his name before the client signed hers. Why should he tempt a client to make off with a check before Max had a chance to take his share?

Whatever the reason, the check couldn't be negotiated now. Mike turned to his partner, a trim young man in his early forties.

"Tim, you could help her, couldn't you? This is your area. Can't someone be appointed to handle things like this over in the Surrogate's Court?"

He handed the check to Tim, who glanced at it and looked back at him.

"Sure, Mike. That would be Max's executor, assuming he had a Will. Otherwise, his administrator. But either way, his family would have to get involved, and he's been here such a short time I really don't even know if he was married, much less had any children. Do you, Mrs. Murphy? Or is it Miss?"

"It's Mrs., sir. How do you know my name?"

"Well, I assume the signature on the back of the check is yours, and that's also the other name on the front, along with Mr. Karraten's. I'm Tim O'Leary, and this is Mike Green. He and I own this building and have the office right next door. So, what happened here today?"

The lady looked like she was about to break into tears again, but she took a deep breath and started to describe her visit to Karraten's office.

"I had a car accident a few years ago. I live in Co-op City. I was coming up I-95, on my way home after seeing a matinee at one of the theaters in Manhattan. I was almost there when a young kid in a fancy convertible swerved in front of me to get off the road at the Orchard Beach exit. He clipped my front left fender so hard he sent me into a spin, and I lost control and smashed into the exit sign. My car was totaled, and my arm was broken. I spent the night in the hospital and was laid up for days afterwards. I missed so much work, I lost my job.

"Someone told me to call Max, and I did. He helped me sue the driver and his father, who owned the convertible, and he got me a settlement for thirty thousand dollars. That's the check."

"Max was working on a contingency?" Tim said.

"Yes. Max's share was ten thousand, and the rest was mine. I really need it. I'm a secretary, and like I told you, I lost my job because of the broken arm. I'm looking for work now, but I'm way behind on my rent and my landlord is threatening to evict me. What will I do?"

Tim and Mike looked at each other.

"Did you say you lived near here, Mrs. Murphy?" Tim said.

"Yes, right down in Co-op City, just south of here," she said.

"How fast can you type?"

"About sixty words per minute, Mr. O'Leary. Why?"

"Well, our main secretary left last week for her maternity leave, and we're using temps while she's gone. We also have Mrs. Turner, but she's a part-timer, with three school age kids to look after. No way she can do full time. If you're interested, would you mind taking a typing test?"

"Oh, certainly. Can I take it now?"

So Mrs. Murphy was able to pay the rent. An advance on her salary took care of that, and some heavy-duty overtime for the law firm of Green and O'Leary put her back on her financial feet, at least until the firm's regular secretary returned.

Max Karraten did indeed have a Will, and a wife, and three children as well. In short order, his Will was probated, his wife was appointed executor of his estate, and the settlement check was negotiated and deposited, after which his fee got paid and Mrs. Murphy received her share. Tim and Mike's secretary had by then delivered her baby, but after due consideration of her husband's recent promotion and the joys of stay-at-home motherhood, she decided not to return to the office, and Mrs. Murphy's position became permanent. From Max's tragedy had come Mrs. Murphy's salvation.

A happy ending, indeed.

But, as is often the case, the story didn't end there. Or, as Mike, paraphrasing W.B. Yeats, later reminded Tim when they talked about the case, "Being Irish, she had an abiding sense of tragedy, which sustained her through temporary periods of joy."

— 3 —

AS IT TURNED OUT, Madeline Murphy, although indeed known to the world as Mrs. Murphy, was not married. She had been, of course, at one time. Although she and her husband had later divorced, she chose to keep her married name and the prefix "Mrs."

They had one child, a son with the unusual name "Hannibal." After a relatively undistinguished, albeit at times briefly stellar, academic career, Hannibal had pursued various unconventional interests with passion, but without financial success.

And now he was missing.

All of this came to light one summer afternoon when Tim's wife, Marge, drove to Westchester and stopped by the office to drop off some papers Tim had forgotten that morning. More sensitive to such things than her husband, and perhaps because of her long experience as a private investigator, she noticed a sadness about Mrs. Murphy, as the lady worked at her typewriter. Remembering that Mrs. Murphy always seemed to be called by that name, rather than something more familiar like "Madeline" or "Maddy," that was how Marge addressed her.

"Mrs. Murphy, are you okay?"

"Oh yes, hi, Mrs. O'Leary. I'm fine, thank you," she said, still typing.

Marge persisted. "You seem a little blue."

Mrs. Murphy continued to type.

"Nothing important. I was just thinking about my son."

"Is he ill?"

"I don't know."

"Mrs. Murphy, I don't mean to pry, but I'd like to help if I can. Would you like to talk about it? Why don't you stop typing for a minute? Take a break."

Mrs. Murphy didn't stop, but a tear rolled down her cheek.

"Oh, you are upset. Why don't you stop typing? Really. Just for a minute, okay?"

Her fingers finally rested.

"I don't even know where he is."

Over the next twenty minutes, she unburdened herself to Marge, who signaled to Tim to go back into his private office when she saw him start to come out to see what was going on.

Mrs. Murphy said that, quite a while ago and several years after she and her ex-husband were divorced, her son had gone off in search of something that had apparently been of great interest to him. Mrs. Murphy did not fully understand what it was. His contacts became progressively less frequent, and eventually ended completely. While he was gone, his father, her ex-husband Frank, suffered serious injuries in a car accident. He lived in great agony for many months, until he finally passed away.

Frank's Will left everything to Hannibal, but Hannibal's whereabouts were unknown by then. Her former brother-in-law, Chris Murphy, was appointed executor of Frank's estate. He hired a personal injury lawyer, and sued the driver of the other car. The case was settled relatively quickly, for six million dollars, from which the lawyer took two million. Another two million went for taxes, and the rest came into the estate, where it still sat, waiting for Hannibal's return. In the meantime, the brother-in-law had taken executor's commissions, and, since he was also a lawyer, legal fees as well. He had told Mrs. Murphy that he was entitled to both.

The brother-in-law did not like Mrs. Murphy, and never had. She didn't know why, but was more anguished by the fact that he refused to use any of the estate money to hire an investigator to search for Hannibal. This, Chris said, would be "an inappropriate expenditure of estate funds," since, in his opinion at least, Hannibal "obviously values his privacy."

Mrs. Murphy stopped, unable to continue, and stood. She dabbed the tears from her eyes with a tissue, and asked Marge to excuse her so she could go to the ladies' room and compose herself. She almost ran to the door.

Marge rushed into Tim's office.

"Tim, we've got to do something."

"About what?"

"About Mrs. Murphy. Her son is missing!"

"Her son? I didn't know she had children. She didn't mention any when she filled out her tax form. How did you find out about it?"

"It was just now. When I came in, I saw her typing, as usual, but I thought she looked depressed about something. I said so, and asked her what was wrong. She didn't want to talk about it at first, but when I finally got her to open up, she spilled it all out. And then she became so emotional she practically ran out of the office."

"Is she coming back? I'd hate to lose her."

Good secretaries were hard to find.

"Tim, this isn't about the office. She needs our help."

"Okay, sorry. Has she called the police?"

"No, it's not like that. Her son has been missing for a few years. About all I know is that he went off somewhere in search of answers to something. He stayed in touch for a while, but less and less as time went by, and then the calls and letters stopped. Mrs. Murphy hasn't heard from him in over three years. To me that sounds like he may have fallen in with the wrong people, or at least some strange ones."

"What are we supposed to do?"

"I think it's what am I supposed to do, given my profession. But this might require travel, and we don't have anyone to watch the kids. Even so, you're a lawyer, and I'm an investigator. Between the two of us, we should be able to figure out a way to find out where he is. I feel so sorry for Mrs. Murphy."

"Whoa, Marge, whoa. Slow down. Who says her son wants to be found? And what if he doesn't? I can understand that she misses him, but it sounds like he might just be trying to see the world, exploring. Did she say he might be in danger from something?"

"No, just that he might be homeless, living on the street, and that he'd be so much safer if he could at least get a place of his own."

"So she wants him to move back in with her?"

"No. A place of his own."

"But he couldn't afford that. You said he might be homeless."

"His father left him money."

"How much?"

"Well, it sounds like there could be at least two million, sitting in an estate account waiting for him, while Mrs. Murphy's brother-in-law siphons off fees and commissions for himself and his law office, and makes no effort whatsoever to find Hannibal."

"Hannibal?"

"Yes, that's her son's name."

"Why doesn't Hannibal tell him to turn it over?"

"Because Hannibal doesn't know it exists. His father was still alive when he took off."

"Listen, Marge, we'd better talk about this tonight. I

have an appointment in fifteen minutes. They're dividing up the assets in the Casey Estate. You know—the one with the brother and sister who hate each other."

"That sounds like a few of them. Good luck."

"Thanks. I'll need it."

— 4 —

"SORRY, I'M LATE. How is everybody this afternoon?"

The answer to this question was obvious, as evidenced by his client Alfred Casey's dour expression and the hate-filled stare emanating from the other side of the waiting room, where his client's sister Bridget sat waiting.

"May I speak to you, Mr. O'Leary?" This from his client.

"Sure, Al. Why don't we step out into the hallway for a minute?"

As he opened the door, he looked at the receptionist.

"Miss, could you tell Mr. Zanger we'll be ready to go as soon as I finish speaking to Mr. Casey? We shouldn't be long."

"Certainly, Mr. O'Leary." She reached for the intercom.

Once in the hallway, Tim asked Alfred if he was ready with his selections. The procedure agreed on in advance was to flip a coin, with the winning sibling to get first pick from their mother's personal effects. These consisted primarily of some fine pieces of jewelry, a few valuable works of art, and an antique sterling silver tea service, as well as miscellaneous items of little or no monetary value. Given the significant worth of some of the premium items, it had also been agreed that the loser of the coin flip would get the next two picks, after which the siblings would alternate until all of the personal items were spoken for.

That the siblings had no love for one another was an understatement. As innocuous as this procedure might have sounded to anyone unfamiliar with their family dynamics, it had been agreed upon not only after bitter negotiations involving their attorneys, but also some serious arm-twisting by a member of the Surrogate's Court's law department.

"Mr. O'Leary, my sister really despises me."

"Yes, Al. I think we all know that. It's a shame."

"But, I need to tell you what she's likely to do if she wins the coin toss."

"I assume she'll pick the most valuable item. That's the antique silver tea service. The appraiser put a $20,000 value on it. Nothing else came in over $5,000."

"Right, but only if she thinks it's what I want. If she thinks I want something else, then she'll take that instead, just to hurt me. I know my sister."

"But she'd only be hurting herself."

"It wouldn't matter."

"Well, that's her problem, then, but I don't see what we can do about it."

"That's why I wanted to talk to you. We have to throw her off the track. We have to make her think I want something else, not the tea service."

"Okay. Do you?"

"Yes. There's a little red bicycle over in a corner in the picture of the 'miscellaneous items of no intrinsic market value' on the last page of the appraiser's report. You can't see it in the picture, but there's a small brass plate on the top tube, the tube that runs from the handlebar post to the seat post. The plate is inscribed 'My little guy riding high.' The bike was under our Christmas tree the year I finally learned to ride a bike without training wheels. I forgot about it as I grew older, but I guess my parents kept it for sentimental reasons, out in the garage, all these years. That's what I want."

"So, what's the problem? Your sister certainly wouldn't want it."

"Don't kid yourself, Mr. O'Leary. To my sister, losing a $20,000 silver tea service is nothing compared to being able to really hurt me, so if she thinks I've got my heart set on something besides the tea set, she'll grab whatever it is. I just want her to think that I do want something else, the Sargent painting, but not that it's the bicycle."

"My God, Al! That sounds awful. Are you sure about this?"

"Absolutely. So, what we must do when we go back in there is make her think I'm trying to trick her into taking the silver tea set, and what I really want for myself is one of the paintings. That's what she'll grab if she has a chance, so we have to send a message, but not the right message. I've given this a lot of thought. Here's how we'll do it."

Ten minutes later, they went back into the office.

"We're ready to go, miss. Please tell Mr. Zanger."

"He's waiting for you in the conference room, Mr. O'Leary. His client is in there too. He said you should go right in and join them as soon as you were ready."

Zanger and Al's sister were sitting at the conference table as Tim and Al entered. Zanger smiled. Bridget scowled.

"So, Tim, shall we get right to the coin toss?"

"In a second, Marty. Could we have a quick look at the appraisal first?"

"Sure, it's right over there on the side table. Be my guest."

Al brushed past Tim and picked up the folder. He flipped it open and thumbed through the pages, pausing a few times to study the photos and mumble a comment or two, and then absently glancing at the page with the photo of the silver tea service. Turning his back to his sister, he pointed to the price under the photo, and in a stage whisper, murmured "Look at this one, Mr. O'Leary. Can you imagine that the guy I mentioned, the one who's into this stuff, said this thing would go for twice that much? What was the appraiser thinking when he came up with this number? Beautiful, isn't it?"

Flipping through a few more pages, he pointed to another photo and, rolling his eyes, whispered, "This is it? This is what you were talking about? The John Singer Sargent painting? The consolation prize? I don't know what your friend sees in it, but if worse comes to worst, I'll take it. At least I know I can get rid of it."

"Al, relax. It's a coin toss, fifty-fifty. My money's on you. Win or lose, at least you have options."

Tim had played his part. Now it was his client's turn, his voice rising slightly, as he feigned exasperation.

"That's not what Vince Lombardi said, Mr. O'Leary. I told you."

Bridget snarled, her rather limited patience finally exhausted. She shouted from across the table. "Listen, Alfie, you bozo. I'm not going to sit here forever. The sooner I don't have to be in the same room with you, the better. Let's go."

"Take it easy, Bridget. Just take it easy, will you?"

"Don't you tell me what to do, Alfie."

Bridget started to get out of her chair, but Zanger intervened.

"Okay, okay, everybody settle down. Are we ready to go, Tim?"

"All set, Marty. Al, why don't we sit on this side of the table?" He gestured toward the side opposite Zanger and Bridget.

"Marty, do you have a coin?"

Marty held up a silver dollar.

"This okay?"

"Fine."

"Okay. I've done my part. You get to pick heads or tails, as we agreed."

"Al would like tails."

"Then here goes." Zanger flipped the coin and it landed

on the table, bounced once, wobbled, and settled. Heads.

"Heads it is," said Zanger. "You have first choice, Bridget. Then your brother will get two choices, after which you'll alternate. Would you like to see the appraisal folder?"

"I won't need to, Marty. I know what I want."

Al leaned forward nervously. Bridget put on her nastiest face.

"I want that stupid red bicycle. I've waited years to get the chance to run my car over it."

"No! Bridget. No!"

"Yes, you jerk. Yes! You didn't really think I'd buy your little act. Did you?"

And so went the rest of the afternoon.

Ah, the joys of estate work.

"WHAT AN ORDEAL. Sibling rivalry at its worst." Tim sipped his drink as he and Marge watched the evening news. Their son Timmy was in the kitchen doing his homework, and their daughter Katie sat on the floor tearing pages out of her new coloring book.

"Why does the sister hate him so much?"

"She thinks he was the favorite and she was ignored."

"That's sad. Why did their parents act that way?"

"Who says they did? That's just her version of the truth. I'm not saying that my guy is a saint, but I don't see any sign of favoritism in the mother's Will. The personal effects and the rest of the estate are both divided equally between the two of them, although her share of the residue is to be held in trust. Even there, though, I can see the reason. The daughter has been through three marriages and two personal bank-ruptcies. Putting her share in trust sounds like something a protective parent would do, and at least the mother was sen-sitive enough to name a bank, and not her son, as executor of the estate and as trustee of the trust."

"He should be thankful for that."

"Absolutely. So how was your day?"

"Nothing new and exciting, but I kept thinking about Mrs. Murphy and her son."

"I don't think there's anything we can do about that, Marge. It's sad, but it's really none of our business."

"No, it is our business. She's alone and she needs help. And we're the only ones she has."

"What could we do, even if we wanted to?"

"We could look for him. If I could get some idea of the type of person he is, what his interests are, what he did in the time leading up to his disappearance. Then maybe we could pick up the trail and follow it. He had to have left traces as he drifted away."

"I guess. Why don't you talk to her? Get a little background. You're usually too busy during the week, but she'll be in the office Saturday morning. Mike is wrapping up a litigation matter, and he asked her to come in then to help him catch up on a few things. It should only be for a few hours. Maybe you could take her to lunch."

"Great. I'll do it. Want to join us?"

"I would, Marge, but I can't. I have a golf lesson that day."

"Golf? You don't play golf."

"That's true, but I'd like to try, and some of my friends say it might be good for business. It can't be that tough. After all, I played a lot of baseball when I was a kid, and I was a pretty good hitter. In baseball, that means hitting a moving target. In golf, the ball just sits there, waiting for you to hit it. How hard could it be?"

"I guess, but how could something like golf be good for business?"

"You know, meeting people at the country club, people who need a lawyer for their estate planning, or who want someone they can trust to handle sensitive matters with discretion, like a family dispute over a Will—stuff like that."

"But we don't belong to a country club."

"Maybe it's time to join. There's that club Father Geraghty took me to when I was trying to decide whether to leave the firm in the city, and go out on my own with Mike. The one they call CCD. They have a pool for the kids, and tennis courts, a restaurant and a bar, and of course, golf. I think it would be nice for us."

"Sounds like you've already made up your mind."

"Well, I guess I have. That's where I've been taking lessons, and they've suggested we apply for membership. They're going to show me around the course soon. It's exciting."

"It's certainly tempting, but let's talk about it later. In the meantime, would you ask Mrs. Murphy tomorrow if she'll have lunch with me next Saturday?"

"I'll do that."

"THIS IS QUITE A TREAT for me, Mrs. O'Leary. I don't get to go out to lunch very often."

"Please call me Marge, Mrs. Murphy. After all, we're not in the office now."

"Oh, I don't think so. I'm so used to calling you Mrs. O'Leary. I wouldn't feel comfortable addressing you any other way."

"All right, but any time you want to change, just do so. Now, why don't we relax and have a nice lunch. Maybe you could tell me a little about yourself. I'm interested to know how you became a legal secretary. Did you study somewhere?"

"Yes, at Katharine Gibbs. White gloves and all."

"Are the white gloves still mandatory?"

Mrs. Murphy laughed.

"No, not anymore, but good manners and appropriate attire are. It's an excellent training ground for a secretary, legal or otherwise."

"Did you study at Gibbs before you married?"

"Yes, but I didn't work for long after that. When we had

a baby, my husband and I agreed I should be a stay-at-home mom. That's what I did for a good long while, but then there was the divorce. I knew I'd need an income. My husband and I weren't very well off, and of course there was my son to think of. I took a refresher course and went back to work."

"Was your son living with you?"

"With me most of the time, but he did stay with his father on alternate weekends. He was already a teenager when my husband and I split up, so it wasn't necessary that anyone be home in the daytime, but Frank often traveled for work during the week, and both of us felt Hannibal shouldn't be left alone at night."

"Don't take this the wrong way, Mrs. Murphy, but the name Hannibal is a bit unusual. Was it a family name?"

"Actually, no. My husband's given name was Francis, but he didn't want our son to be a 'junior.' He had some interest in history. He had read about the Carthaginians' famous leader, Hannibal, the one who crossed the Alps to attack Rome. My husband thought the name projected strength, and was a good one for a boy. I went along, but of course couldn't get myself to call a little baby something like Hannibal, so I started calling him 'Hanny.' Then when he was able to say a few words, he thought I was saying 'Honey.' I liked that, of course, so from then on it was 'Honey' for me."

"And for your husband?"

"He still called him Hannibal."

"Was Hannibal a good student? Did he go to college?"

"Yes and no. He'd do well for a while, and then seem to lose interest. Hanny attended three colleges, sometimes in the summer, over two and a half years. He took quite a few courses in history and archaeology, and did eventually graduate, but not from the college he went to first, or the one he went to after that. It was community college where he finished, although with only two years of credits, receiving an associate's a degree in general studies. Hanny said he knew enough to pursue what he wanted, and didn't need what he referred to as 'another piece of paper to hang on the wall' in order to do it."

"Sounds like an interesting young guy."

"That he is. Oh, here's the waitress again. I guess we should order."

"Yes, let's do that. You must be hungry. Tim said you had to be in the office at eight this morning."

They ordered lunch and then talked about the office for a while. Mrs. Murphy was especially interested in the fact that Tim and Mike had started out at a large Manhattan law firm. She said it must have taken a lot of courage to leave a safe harbor like that and strike out on their own. She knew those ventures didn't always end in success. The thought brought her back to the subject of Hannibal.

"Every time he came up with an idea for a new venture, he'd get very excited, jumping in with both feet, talking about nothing else, and hurling himself into it with a vengeance. Eventually, though, the initial thrill would wear off, practical obstacles would crop up, and the project would be abandoned. You had to admire him, though. Whenever something didn't work out, off he'd go in a new direction. Then, at one point, he got excited about archeological discoveries, and how they all pointed to the excesses of rulers, and to the ultimate reckoning of a supreme being."

"You mean God?"

"Yes, that's the way I took it, but he never referred to God. He used the term 'supreme being,' and refused to elaborate. My son insisted that science would eventually yield the answer to that question, but he 'wasn't there yet.'"

"How far had he gotten?"

"Well, he said that many major archaeological sites involved impressive human accomplishments. It seemed, though, that they were always achieved on the backs of enslaved people, who had no choice but to give their short lives to wealthy and powerful rulers. Their efforts, he said, could not be rewarded while the oppressors remained alive, so the supreme being had to remove the despots from the scene of their self-glorification. Then the descendants of the exploited ones could enjoy what their ancestors had created, without fear of the oppressors, and they could admire their own ancestors for what they had built. As time went by, we could do so as well, as could, perhaps, those who had done the work."

"The workers? So, Hannibal believed in an afterlife?"

"I think so, in a sense. He may have just felt that the workers knew that their abusers, and others like them, would someday be gone, and that what they were building would live on. He would say that it was the supreme being's revenge, giving these beautiful things to us, and to the builders themselves, and to their descendants, after it took the lives of the evil ones away from them."

"It?"

"Yes. 'It.' My son never assigned a gender to what he called the supreme being."

"That's fascinating. Was he planning to teach?"

"He was, in fact, but his ideas didn't generate much enthusiasm among the college administrators he approached, looking for employment as an instructor or as a guest lecturer. They regarded Hanny as either something of a crackpot or a religious zealot. In any event, they had no interest in putting someone with only an associate's degree on their faculty. So, he finally gave up and decided to focus on cosmology."

"Cosmology? You mean the study of the origins of the universe?"

"Yes. Have you heard of it?"

"Actually, I have, Mrs. Murphy. A key witness in a case Tim and I worked on about ten years ago was involved in that area at MIT. It sounded awfully complicated."

"It is, or at least I think it is. I could never quite understand what Hanny was saying when he tried to explain his theories to me. He had ultimately realized that the magnificent structures he had been studying, notwithstanding the fact that they had outlived the oppressors, might eventually crumble themselves. He decided that if that were the case, he would look for something more permanent. He thought the answer might lie in the study of cosmology. I asked him how he could ever advance in a field like that without further education, but he insisted he could learn it on his own. He said he had attended a lecture about cosmology once. When the speaker tried to explain why cosmologists believe the universe is 13.8 billion years old, he droned on for so long that Hanny was convinced it would be 13.9 billion years before the lecture ended. So, he got up and left. I'm afraid school was not my son's thing."

"And I assume that didn't lead to a job either, did it?"

"No, it didn't, Mrs. O'Leary."

— 7 —

BY THE TIME LUNCH ENDED, Marge had learned almost every-thing there was to know about Hannibal Murphy, with one significant exception–where he was now.

His mother said Hanny had become intrigued by a new scientific concept called "dark energy." He believed it might tie his other theories together, allowing him to devise a "grand unified theory." This, he said, was another new con-cept, which brilliant physicists were seeking to formulate, but which he thought was not to be found through pure-ly scientific analysis. Instead, he suspected, there might be a connection between this mysterious energy and the workings of the same supreme being he believed to be instrumental in the righting of wrongs perpetrated on the weak by the strong. Such a combination of astounding breakthroughs would catapult him to the apex of the scientific community, earning him well deserved acclaim, to say nothing of paid lecturing engagements at scientific conferences and univer-sities everywhere. In order to accomplish this ambitious ob-jective, he had told his parents, he would have to travel and study extensively, obviously at significant expense, at least some of which he had hoped they would cover.

His father resisted, telling his son that the time had come to go to work and earn a living. To settle down to a normal way of life, like the rest of the world.

"I understand young men have dreams," Mr. Murphy said, "but you need to face reality, and accept the more sedate existence that comes with maturity, however unexciting that might seem."

Mrs. Murphy, however, succumbed, agreeing to underwrite "this last adventure, Honey." She gave Hannibal the balance of her savings from the divorce settlement, and made him promise to stay in touch.

"You always have a place to come home to if things don't work out," she said.

So, Hannibal set off in search of proof of his theories. He first wished to see for himself how well the monuments men had built to themselves had withstood the ravages of time. This, he said, would require journeying west, and then south to Central and South America. As time progressed, his calls became less and less frequent and, after he mailed his mother a note from somewhere in Peru, he was not heard from again. That had been three years ago, a year before his father died in the auto accident.

Mrs. Murphy was beside herself by this time, especially after she became aware of the AIDS epidemic that had begun sweeping the country in recent years. Although she believed Hannibal was unlikely to have contracted it by conventional means, she had heard about other ways one could become infected. These included giving blood, which Hannibal had done on a number of occasions when he needed money. Marge assured her that getting infected in this manner wasn't possible, since all of the equipment used in extracting blood from donors was sterilized in advance, and discarded after use. Mrs. Murphy still worried, not sure the same adherence to safe medical procedures was standard practice in the countries her son was visiting.

"Why doesn't he call? He could reverse the charges."

"From Peru?"

"Or send me a letter."

There was no way to put Mrs. Murphy at ease with the situation, and Marge couldn't blame her. In the end, she decided to try and find Hannibal herself.

"Mrs. Murphy, I think you know that I'm a private investigator. This isn't my typical type of case, but some of the same methods might work here. Would you be willing to answer some questions?"

"Of course. Anything."

"Okay. Where did Hanny go first?"

"He went west, and then south. He started in Colorado, where he wanted to view Pueblo cliff dwellings in a place named Mesa Verde. He said they weren't equivalent to the towering structures later built in Central and South America. But he thought they might be a good starting point for his research. He felt they might provide a clue as to how something that starts as a productive use of natural materials to build homes for people can devolve into the construction of monuments to vanity. He said the same process that resulted in the creation of the temples in the Americas may have led, thousands of years earlier, to the rise of the Egyptian dynastic structures, such as the pyramids.

"Then he went to Mexico, after that to Guatemala and, eventually, to Peru. He was entranced by the history of the Mayans, the Incas and the Aztecs, all of whom, he thought, probably started out constructing useful architecture like the Pueblo people, but then developed into builders of temples for self-glorification, and even human sacrifice, a moral corrosion to which he attributed their eventual downfall."

"When he called, was he upbeat about the progress he was making?"

"He was excited at first, but after a while he started sounding frustrated, and he was running out of money. Hanny spoke a little Spanish, so he was able to get work here and there, but the jobs paid next to nothing. I begged him to come home, but he said he had to keep trying. He ... I'm sorry, I can't ... I have to stop."

Mrs. Murphy started to sob.

Marge reached across the table and patted her hand.

"It's all right, Mrs. Murphy, don't cry. We'll find him somehow. Don't worry."

8

TIM PUT DOWN THE NEWSPAPER and looked up from his Sunday morning bacon and eggs breakfast.

"How did things go with Mrs. Murphy yesterday?"

"Well, she's upset, and she has every right to be. Her son, somewhere in South America, probably out of money. Three years since she's heard from him. What if it were Timmy? I wouldn't be able to sleep at night."

"Think you can find him?"

"I really don't know. Maybe I should go into my office today and make some calls. I have a directory of foreign embassies. Some of them might be open on Sunday. Maybe they can help. Could you watch the kids?"

"Sorry. No can do. I'm supposed to play golf this morning. Remember what I told you about joining a club? Well, the pro at the club said he thinks I should try playing a round there."

"Does he know your experience level?" Marge looked worried.

"He says I have a long way to go, but it's time to 'get my feet wet.' He ordered a set of clubs for me, and arranged for one of the members to take me out and show me the course today. Better go, I'm due over there at nine. Leave the dishes in the sink. I'll clean up when I get back. See you later."

Tim got up, gave Marge a quick kiss, and left the house, visibly excited.

The Country Club of Darien, or "CCD," as the members called it, was only a few miles from their house. Tim arrived well ahead of his 9:00 a.m. tee time, planning to warm up on the practice tee for a while first.

Everything went downhill from there.

Still excited, but a little nervous, Tim stopped by the clubhouse so he could put on his golf shoes, but soon realized he had forgotten to bring them. He raced back to his car and drove home. Hurrying into the house, he practically tripped over Marge, who was playing a board game with the children on the living room floor.

"Back already?"

"Forgot my golf shoes."

He took the stairs two at a time and rushed into the bedroom, finding the shoes next to his dresser. He snatched them up, ran out to the car, started it up, and gunned the engine. It was twenty minutes to nine when he arrived at the club again, leaving him just enough time to put on the golf shoes, grab his new clubs, and hit a few balls out on the practice tee before 9:00.

But where were his clubs? The golf shop, of course! He hurried in and approached the counter. Somewhat out of breath, Tim identified himself to the attendant and requested the clubs.

"Mr. O'Leary, is it? I understand you may be joining the club. That's wonderful. Your new clubs should be here in a few weeks."

"You mean they're not here?"

"You just ordered them yesterday, didn't you?"

"Right. They're not here yet?"

"Well, no. It takes at least a few weeks for them to arrive

from the manufacturer."

This was getting scary.

"The manufacturer? I thought you would just pick them up in town."

"I'm sorry. You must have misunderstood. We fitted you for a custom set, which had to be ordered. When do you need them?"

Tim looked at his watch.

"My tee time is in ten minutes."

"Oh, my! Well, we can help with that. I'll call over to the bag room and ask them for one of our rental sets. Are you riding or walking?"

"Riding or walking? Do you mean how did I get here? I drove over. Where is the bag room? Is it far?" Tim checked the time again. He was starting to sweat.

"Oh, no. I'm sorry, Mr. O'Leary. You misunderstand. The 'bag room' is in the next building. It's where we keep our members' golf bags. They'll bring the clubs over here for you. They just need to know if they should put them on a motorized golf cart or on a pushcart. That's why I said, 'riding or walking?' Who are you playing with today?"

"I don't know. Tony said he'd arrange it."

"Tony the golf pro?"

"Yes."

"All right, Mr. O'Leary, let me check." He picked up the phone and started making calls. Tim kept checking his watch.

"Mr. O'Leary?"

Tim looked up.

"You'll be playing with Mr. DeMarco this morning. The starter says Mr. DeMarco is waiting for you on the first tee, and his clubs are already on a motorized cart. We'll send a set of clubs over there for you, and they'll be put on the cart with his, so the two of you can ride together. Have a good round!"

"Thanks. It's my first."

Tim left the shop and hurried toward the first tee, where he saw a distinguished looking middle-aged gentleman chat-

ting with a younger man who wore a staff member's golf
shirt. Looking over, the older man called out to Tim.

"Hello, there! You must be Tim O'Leary."

"Yes, sir. I am. Are you Mr. DeMarco?"

"Yes, indeed. Paul DeMarco. Welcome to the club, and
say hello to Jack Curlew, our starter. I understand you and
I are playing with one another this morning. Ready to go?"

"I suppose so. I was going to warm up, but I got a little
confused about a couple of things and didn't have time.
I guess it doesn't matter. Did they tell you this is my first
time out?"

"Yes, they did, Tim. They asked if I'd show you around
the course, and I said it would be my pleasure. Where did
you play previously?"

"No, I mean this is my first time out anywhere. I'm just
learning the game."

DeMarco looked surprised.

The starter grinned.

"Mr. DeMarco, should I let your wife know you might be
a little late for lunch?"

DeMarco gave a little laugh.

"Don't mind him, Tim. Those must be your clubs. They
just came over from the bag room. Why don't you tee off
first? The first tee is right over here. Keep your head down
and your eye on the ball. I'll watch where it goes."

Tim reached into the indicated bag of clubs, took one,
and walked toward the tee.

"Say, won't you be needing your driver?"

Tim looked down and realized he was holding a putter.
Quickly shoving it back in the bag, he selected the largest
club and walked up onto the tee, but suddenly remembered
he had forgotten to bring any golf balls with him.

"Uh, Mr. DeMarco?"

"Paul, Tim. Call me Paul."

"Right. Sorry. Paul. I forget to bring a ball."

Curlew burst out laughing. DeMarco tried not to.

"No problem, Tim. I have plenty. Take a few of mine." He reached into his own bag and pulled out several brand-new golf balls, handing them, along with a few tees, to Tim.

"Now you're all set."

Tim took the balls, put one of them on a tee, and stuck it into the ground. Standing up, he gripped the golf club with both hands in the manner the pro had instructed during his lessons. He leaned forward, settled the club head against the ball, and got ready to swing.

The ball fell off the tee.

"That's one, Mr. O'Leary!" Curlew was really enjoying himself now.

DeMarco intervened again.

"Cut it out, will you Jack? Now just relax, Tim. This is a difficult game, but it can be a lot of fun once you get the hang of it. Put the ball back on the tee and take a nice easy swing at it."

Tim did as he was told, up to the easy swing part. Remembering his success hitting baseballs, he took a mighty lunge at the little ball.

And missed.

"Strike one!" Curlew thrust out his right arm in the fashion of a home plate umpire.

"Jack, please. Relax, Tim. Try again. Easy this time."

Tim looked down, thought of escaping, managed to resist the temptation, and took a tentative swing at the ball.

He connected, and the ball actually flew off the tee and soared out toward the fairway, albeit for only about fifty yards.

"Okay! Six more of those and you're on the green." Curlew again.

"Just ignore him, Tim. Let me hit off and we'll be on our way."

DeMarco teed up his own ball, stepped back, and drove it over 200 yards straight down the fairway. He looked over his shoulder at the starter.

"Show's over, Jack. Sorry to disappoint you, but we'll have to go now. Come on, Tim, hop in the cart and we'll be on our way."

The rest of the round confirmed Tim's growing realization that hitting a stationery golf ball would not be as simple an exercise as he had originally assumed. When he finally reached the thirteenth hole, he came to a new understanding of what the pro might have unwittingly been predicting when he suggested that it was time for Tim to "get his feet wet." The thirteenth hole, it turned out, was aptly associated with that unlucky number.

Tim's version of a drive skidded off the tee, went briefly airborne, bounced, and rolled toward, and then over, the edge of a level area just beyond the place from which he had struck the ball. This place, Paul DeMarco had explained earlier, was called the tee box.

"Pick that one up, Tim. We'll drop it on the fairway, and you can hit it from there. Don't want to hold up the group behind us!"

DeMarco started the golf cart and drove along the path next to the tee box, as Tim hurried ahead to retrieve the ball, looking for it as he crossed a little bridge that connected the tee box to the fairway. Seeing the ball at the edge of a slight decline, he quickened his pace and started to jog down to get it.

"Careful, Tim, that spot gets slippery from the water sprinklers. Watch yourself. Oh, no!"

Tim had slipped on some wet leaves, tried to regain his balance, tripped on his golf ball, and tumbled headfirst into a pond that lay at the foot of the slope. Soaked and muddy, he stood up, reached back and picked up his ball.

"Got it, Paul!"

9

ALTHOUGH DEMARCO SUGGESTED calling it a day, Tim declined and they forged ahead, completing the round an hour and a half later. To Tim's surprise, his own game improved, and he actually managed to make a few decent shots as they went along. By the time they finished, his clothes had dried, although they were still caked with mud, as were his face and his hair. DeMarco shook his hand, apparently the customary thing for gentlemen to do at the end of a shared round of golf.

"We'll have to do this again, Tim," he said.

Tim assumed the comment also to be customary, although probably not a suggestion he should take literally.

Marge was outside with the children when he got back home.

"My God, Tim! What happened to you?"

"Took a spill. Landed in a pond."

"What does that have to do with playing golf?"

"There's a lot about golf I didn't know. It's a long story."

"Well, maybe you should take a shower first, and get cleaned up. Then you can tell me about it, but first let me share an idea I had for tracking down Hanny."

"Hanny? Who's that?"

"Mrs. Murphy's son. His name is Hannibal, but she calls him Hanny, or sometimes Honey."

"Ahh. Okay."

"He had to have crossed several international borders in order to get to Peru. That's where he was when she last heard from him, and I assume he's crossed a few more since then."

"Is that something you can find out?"

"There must be records kept of such border crossings by the individual countries. I'm going to make some calls and see if I can find which one he entered most recently. That will at least narrow the search, and then I'll try to see if I can find an investigator in that country who can follow his trail from that point on."

"Good luck."

* * *

The next morning, after calls to twelve foreign embassies from her office in New Haven, Marge was ready to give up. Some people who answered the phone were polite, others not, but no one could help. Hannibal had not registered his travel plans with any of their offices, and visa and border crossing information remained private, unless requested by an authorized representative of the United States government, pursuant to treaty. Marge reached the last embassy on her list, the Bolivian Embassy, just before noon. Once she had been connected with an English-speaking representative, she asked the same questions, with the same results. Sighing, she thanked him, and started to hang up.

"Why don't you try CBP? Maybe they can help."

"I'm sorry. CBP?"

"Customs and Border Protection, ma'am."

"Oh. Can you transfer me?"

"No, CBP is in your country. They have records back to 1982."

"Records of what?"

"Of where and when your citizens used their passports when traveling abroad. Of course, that information is protected by the Privacy Act, so not everyone can get it."

"Who can?"

"The person with the passport."

"But that's who I'm looking for. I don't know where he is."

"Are you his lawyer?"

"No, I'm not a lawyer, but my husband is. Can he get it?"

"Did the traveler make him his designated representative for access to that information?"

"No."

"Well, sorry, then. I just thought—"

"No, don't be sorry. At least you tried to help. You're the only one who had any ideas. Everyone else just said there was nothing they could do. I don't think the other embassies even knew about what you've been telling me. How did you learn about it?"

"Oh, I'm actually from the States. I just graduated from college last year, and I wanted to travel some before I settled down back home."

"Sounds very exciting."

"I'm here on a work visa. I had to take a course before I came down, so I could get this job. That's how I learned about the Privacy Act and CBP and all the other stuff. I even designated my father as my authorized representative, just in case I turned up missing."

"What do you mean 'down here?' Isn't your embassy on 46th Street?"

"Yes, it is, but I'm talking to you on a direct line from La Paz."

"Really? Wow. How did they do that?"

"Technology. It's the latest thing. Who knows what they'll come up with next? Anyway, good luck finding your missing guy."

"Thanks, Mr. ..."

"Carlos. Carlos Villalobos. You can ask for me if you need to call us again."

"Let's hope I won't have to. But thanks again. You've been very helpful. Bye now."

"Adios to you. And buena suerte."

Marge got the 'adios' part, but not the rest.

"Adios to you as well. Gracias."

She hung up, and called Tim's office. Mrs. Murphy answered.

"Green and O'Leary."

"Mrs. Murphy, this is Marge O'Leary."

"Oh, hi. Mr. O'Leary has a client in there now. Shall I tell him you're on the phone?"

"No, Mrs. Murphy. It's you I wanted to speak to."

"Oh, all right. Is anything wrong?"

"No, not at all. Everything's fine. I just wanted to ask you a question. Did your son sign anything before he left that would authorize you to handle his affairs while he was away? You know, like his bank accounts or anything like that?"

"He really didn't have any bank accounts, Mrs. O'Leary. Maybe a small one that had hardly any money in it."

"But didn't you say you gave him the money from your divorce settlement to pay for his travel expenses?"

"Oh, yes, of course, but we used that to buy American Express traveler's checks, so he could exchange them for foreign currency as he moved around."

"So, he didn't sign anything like a power of attorney?"

"No, he didn't."

"Or anything else?"

"The only thing he signed was some paper the attorney I was working for back then had prepared. He said it was a good idea to have one when a person is traveling abroad. I'm not really sure what it's for. It made me a representative or something."

"Do you have it with you, Mrs. Murphy?"

"Well, I think it might be in my desk. I keep things like that here in the office. That way I can get at them during business hours, if I need them. Nothing's open by the time I get home, you know. Or on weekends, of course. Not that I would take care of my personal business during office hours. I do take an hour for lunch, though, so I don't think it's wrong to make a quick trip to the bank then. You know I would never—"

"I'm sure you wouldn't, Mrs. Murphy, but would you mind taking a look for that paper now? Perhaps you could call me back if you find it."

"Of course. Right away."

Marge hung up, and looked at her notes while she waited. Ten minutes later the phone rang.

"Yes, Mrs. O'Leary, I found it. It's a little crumpled up. Just a second. Okay, it says I'm an 'Accredited Representative' and then something about Form G-639, whatever that is."

Marge laughed with excitement.

"Mrs. Murphy, that's exactly what we need! It might help us find out which countries Hanny visited, and when. Could you give it to my husband, so he can show it to me when I get home tonight?"

"I'll do that as soon as his conference is over. Do you really think it might work? I mean, we know he was in Peru. What if it he's not there anymore?"

"That's the point, Mrs. Murphy. The man at the Bolivian Embassy said what you have can be used to find out when your son went through Customs and Immigration in the different countries he visited. If he left Peru, it means he went to another country, and if he left that country, then he went to another one, and so on, until he entered a country where there's no record he has left yet. That's the country he's in now."

"Would it say where he is in that country?"

"I'm afraid not, but at least that would narrow it down. It would give us a starting point for going further."

"Do you think there would be a way to find him then?"

"We'll find a way, Mrs. Murphy."

Marge wished she was more confident that this would prove to be the case, but better to stay upbeat.

"Oh, that would be wonderful! I'm so worried about him. Thank you, Mrs. O'Leary. Thank you."

Marge hung up, praying that she hadn't given Mrs. Murphy false hope. So what if they discovered what country he was in now? Finding him within any given country, investigator or not, was still a very long shot.

10

MARGE AND TIM HELPED MRS. MURPHY apply for Hanny's travel records from The US Citizenship and Immigration Services, to whom they'd been referred by CBP. Weeks passed. Tim played less golf, and started talking about taking up tennis, thinking a moving target might suit him better. Marge suggested they wait until next season before considering joining the country club. The kids started getting ready for school, and thoughts about Hannibal Murphy receded into the background.

Until one day at Tim's office, when Mrs. Murphy shrieked and jumped up from her desk.

"He's back!"

She nearly knocked over a cup of coffee next to the pile of mail at her desk.

"Who's back?" Tim had come running out of his office.

"Hanny, Mr. O'Leary! My son. Hanny. I just got a letter from Immigration Services. It says he reentered the United States last month."

Thank God the news is good, Tim thought.

"Do they say where, Mrs. Murphy?"

"Yes, they do. Well, of all places ... Vermont!"

"Vermont?"

"That's what it says."

"From where?"

"It says from someplace in Canada."

"May I see that, Mrs. Murphy?"

"Certainly, here." Her hand trembled as she handed him the paper.

The response from the Customs and Immigration Service was quite detailed, but clearly indicated the arrival of Hannibal Murphy at the Highwater-North Troy border crossing station in Vermont on August 12th, 1987. Prior to that, he had crossed borders in Mexico, several central American countries, and then Columbia, Peru, Bolivia, and Argentina, before appearing to have found his way to Canada by sea. Once he arrived in the U.S., he had stayed put, at least for the time being, since there were no more entries on the report.

"I have to go right now," said Mrs. Murphy, ecstatic. "I have some vacation time left, don't I, Mr. O'Leary?"

"Yes, you do, Mrs. Murphy, but where will you go?"

"Why, Vermont, of course."

"But you don't even know if he's still there. He could be anywhere in the United States. This only shows that he hasn't left the country since then. That means this country, the United States. Even if he is still in Vermont, he could be in any number of places up there."

"Well ... wouldn't he be in the phone book?"

"Probably not yet, and even then, only if he has a telephone. Tell you what. Why don't I call Marge and ask her to look into it? She has access to that kind of thing, and she might have some other ideas also."

"Would you mind? Oh, I just have to know. Thank you. Thank you."

Marge was at her office in New Haven, when Tim called her and told her the news about Hanny being back in the States. Thrilled, she said she had a contact in Vermont and would give him a call. An hour later, she got back to Tim.

"No luck," Marge said. "My friend in Montpelier checked with Vtel, the Vermont Telephone Company. At first, they thought he was joking, because of the Hannibal part. When he convinced them he was serious, they told him there are hundreds of Murphys listed in phone directories around the state, but no Hannibals. They added that Vermont is where the Green Mountains are located, not the Alps, but if they saw any elephants around they'd be sure to call my friend. Otherwise, he might want to take a trip to Italy and check to see if Hannibal is still there."

"I guess they thought it was all very funny."

"I guess so. To tell you the truth, I think my friend did too."

"Any other ideas, Marge?"

"Actually, I do. It's late September, the beginning of foliage season in Vermont. Why don't we take a mini-vacation and drive up there for a week? It's supposed to be beautiful, with the leaves turning, the clear, crisp days, the cozy country inns with logs burning in the hearth. We could ask the nanny to stay at the house and watch Timmy and Katie while we're away."

"What does this have to do with Hannibal?"

"That would be part of it. We can bring Mrs. Murphy along for the first few days, and get her a separate room. After all, we probably wouldn't even recognize Hannibal if we saw him, and she's more likely to have some idea of the kind of places he would be likely to go."

"A few days? How would she get home after that?"

"There are direct flights from Burlington to New York on Eastern Airlines, and they're not too expensive. We could take her to the airport when the time comes for her to head back down to New York. Then we'd be alone for the rest of the week."

Tim thought about his calendar for the next several days, and decided there was nothing that couldn't be moved, or in the case of a golf date the following weekend, nothing he wouldn't be thrilled to cancel. Nightmares of another disaster on the links could be shelved for the time being.

"I love it," he said. "Let me go talk to Mrs. Murphy. Mike can get a temp to cover for her while she's away."

Two days later, Tim and Marge picked up Mrs. Murphy at the Darien train station and started the drive to Vermont. Mrs. Murphy sat in the back seat, and alternated between thanking them for helping her and fretting over the possibility that her son couldn't be found.

"What if he went somewhere else?" she said.

"Well, he might have, Mrs. Murphy, but this is as good a place to start as anywhere," said Marge, trying to be encouraging. "At least we know he was in Vermont six weeks ago."

"So how will we look for him?"

"We thought we'd start up near the Canadian border and work our way down from there over the next few days," Marge said. "We can take the interstates–I-95 as far as New Haven, and then I-91 most of the rest of the way. The trip should be manageable, only about six or seven hours, with a stop or two along the way to stretch our legs and maybe have lunch."

"Where will we be staying?"

"There's supposed to be a nice place not far from where your son entered the States. It's called Jay Peak Resort. We made reservations to stay there tonight. Then we can start looking for Hanny tomorrow."

"Oh, thank you for helping, but I'm so nervous. I can't stop shaking. Do you think he might be sleeping in the woods? I think they have bears up there. And moose. I heard that moose are very dangerous if you get them stirred up. Mountain lions, too! Oh no." She started to cry.

Marge tried to calm her, but without success, so she tried to change the subject.

"I think the only wildlife at Jay Peak are the après skiers, Mrs. Murphy. They say there are some pretty wild parties in the base lodge after the lifts close down."

"Skiers? Is there snow up where we're going, Mrs. O'Leary? I didn't bring my winter clothes."

"No, Mrs. Murphy. I didn't mean now. That's in the winter. Just pretty leaves and crisp evenings. Now why don't you close your eyes and try to rest. We have a long way to go."

Mrs. Murphy dutifully closed her eyes, but sleep wouldn't come. She had forgotten how cold Vermont would be in the wintertime, and that was only months away. Visions of a shivering Hanny up in the mountains now competed with thoughts of ravenous bears hunting for another good meal before settling down to a long winter's hibernation.

11

TIM, MARGE AND MRS. MURPHY arrived at the Hotel Jay late that afternoon. Mrs. Murphy had finally settled down, and she napped a bit in the back seat, after which she chirped happily about the beautiful changing leaves, their colors intensifying as the three travelers made their way further and further north.

Getting out of the car, they entered the hotel, and checked in at the front desk. Two bellhops came to carry their bags, including Mrs. Murphy's surprisingly large suitcase, up to their rooms. When the bellhops arrived, Marge smiled at Mrs. Murphy.

"Let's all settle into our rooms and unpack," Marge said. "If it's all right with you, we can meet in the dining room at seven. That will give us a couple of hours to unwind."

When Tim and Marge entered their room, their eyes went straight to the view of the mountains beyond a deck they could see through glass doors on the far side. Skirting the bed, they opened the doors and stepped outside.

Although the sun had already disappeared behind the mountains to the west, it had not fully set, and its light was bathing some of the mountains to the east in a brilliant radiance, as the changing leaves glowed in its rays. Tim and Marge stood on the deck, taking in the view, as they watched the shadows of the mountains behind them creep up the slopes on the eastern range. Their arms held one another's waists tightly.

"This was a great idea, Marge. It's so beautiful here." He pulled her closer and she leaned into him.

"I've never been to Vermont before, but I'm glad I'm doing it with you."

"Even if we don't find Hanny."

"Why hasn't he even called her? He could have reversed the charges, now that he's back in the States."

"We know he doesn't think the way the rest of us do."

"I guess you're right, but I'm a mother, too, and I know how I would feel. Anyway, we'd better get ready for dinner. We're supposed to meet Mrs. Murphy down in the dining room at seven."

Tim turned and faced Marge, pulling her even closer.

"Maybe we could be a few minutes late. I don't think she'd mind."

They almost stumbled back into the room, falling onto the bed together.

12

MRS. MURPHY WAS SITTING at a table in the hotel's wood paneled dining room. She looked up and smiled as Tim and Marge entered the room.

"What have you two been up to?"

Tim blushed, but Marge smiled back.

"Oh, you know, Mrs. Murphy, just checking out the view while we unpacked our bags."

"Of course. How rude of me." Mrs. Murphy suppressed her smile. "This area is just so beautiful, isn't it?"

They joined her at the table as a young waiter came over.

"Hey, welcome to Jay. How's it going?"

"It's going fine," Marge responded, winking at Mrs. Murphy. "We'd like to have dinner, but maybe a round of drinks first. What would you like, Mrs. Murphy?"

Mrs. Murphy brightened. "Perhaps an aperitif. What do you have?"

That stumped the waiter, whose name was apparently Ryan, given the badge pinned to his shirt.

"Is that some kind of French wine, miss?" Ryan said. "We don't have many of them. There's some up over the border. In Kee-beck, I mean."

"No, no, I'm sorry. It's a before dinner drink, like a Manhattan."

"That's even farther away, ma'am, way down south. No, I don't think we have anything from there."

"Oh, of course. Sure. Well then, what do you have?"

"We have lots of whiskey," Ryan said, on firmer ground now. "Bourbon, rye, scotch, some Canadian whiskey for the folks who come down from there. That kind of thing. And something they call glue-wine."

"Glue what?"

Marge jumped in.

"I think he's talking about something called 'glühwein,' Mrs. Murphy. 'G-l-u-e-h-w-e-i-n. It's red wine mixed with spices, and warmed. Sometimes it's called mulled wine. It's supposed to warm you up after a cold day on the ski slopes. Isn't that so, Ryan?"

"Well, I'm not even sure how to spell it," he said. "It's warm, like you said, and lots of customers drink it during the ski season, but I don't know what it's made from, and I'm not even sure we have any now. I could check. Mostly, though, we have plenty of beer. On tap or by the bottle. Sam Adams is my favorite. It just came out a couple of years ago, and it's made in Boston. Want to try that?"

"Why don't you two order your drinks while I decide?" Mrs. Murphy said.

"That Sam Adams sounds good," Tim said. "Put me down for one of those. How about you, Marge?"

"Why not? I'll have one, too. Mrs. Murphy?"

Mrs. Murphy shrugged her shoulders.

"Well, when in Rome, as they say. Make it three, young man."

Marge laughed.

"Good for you, Mrs. Murphy. This is going to be a fun trip."

Ryan dropped three menus on the table and strolled toward the bar.

Tim looked at Marge, who nodded and spoke to Mrs. Murphy.

"Tim and I thought we'd start up at the border crossing station tomorrow. It's a short drive from here, only about ten miles. Maybe someone in the customs office can give us an idea of where a person like Hanny may have gone from there. We're assuming he was traveling by some form of public transportation."

Mrs. Murphy nodded. "That's true. He certainly couldn't have afforded to rent a car, but you know, he had another way of traveling that worried me sick. He liked to hitchhike."

"I hadn't thought of that," said Tim. "Someone coming down from Canada could have picked him up. One way or the other, we know he crossed the border at North Troy, so that's where we'll go."

Mrs. Murphy picked up one of the menus and started searching for something local, as Ryan returned with a pitcher of Sam Adams and three glasses.

"Here you go."

Tim looked surprised. "A pitcher?"

"Yep. It's cheaper this way. More brew, less buck. Any questions about the menu?"

Mrs. Murphy had a few.

"This all seems very heavy, Mr. Ryan. 'The Whaler—deep fried haddock swimming in fries.' 'Jay's bar-bee-que platter—served over a sky-high pile of fries.' Things like that. Do you have anything lighter?"

"Sure do, ma'am. Look on the next page."

Mrs. Murphy obliged.

"See? Under 'Lighter Side'?"

She looked. And gasped.

" 'Vermont's famous house smoked cheddar burger—one-half pound fresh ground chuck smothered in house smoked cheddar, served on a spicy roll with lettuce, tomato, onion and pickles.' That's on the lighter side?"

"You could have the pickle on the side."

"I don't think so. What's 'venison'?"

"Deer meat."

She gasped. "Like Bambi? How mean. No, I couldn't. Oh, wait. Here's something. But I'm not sure what it is— 'Beefalo burger: fewer calories, less cholesterol and lower in fat than beef burgers. Served with our house salad. Try one and you'll never go back!' My lord! What on earth is a 'beefalo burger?'"

"That's easy, ma'am. It's a cross breed of cattle and buffalo. The latest thing. Order one. Trust me, you'll love it."

"Oh, I guess so. I'll try it. Well done, please. How about you two?"

Enjoying this exchange, Tim and Marge had neglected to study the menu themselves. They glanced at one another, and nodded.

"Beefalo burgers all around, Ryan," Tim said. "Make ours medium rare."

— 13 —

THE NEXT MORNING was cool and pleasant, as the three of them climbed into Tim's car and drove east, and then north, toward the Canadian border. With very little traffic, they arrived in less than twenty minutes, pulling into a parking lot next to a modest building with a sign reading "Highwater" above the words "Douanes" and "Customs." It looked more like a drive-through car wash than the imposing government buildings Tim was used to seeing in New York. Nevertheless, it was the place where Hanny Murphy had come home, or at least to the country that was his home.

Mrs. Murphy couldn't help becoming emotional, dabbing her eyes with a tissue.

"I'm sorry. This is so silly of me, but just knowing my boy was here makes me happy. I feel like I'm finally going to see him again. Can we go inside?"

Marge looked over her shoulder from the front passenger seat. "Of course we can, that's why we're here. Tim, do you have that letter we received from Immigration Services?"

"In my briefcase, Marge. Mrs. Murphy, it's sitting next to you back there. Could you take the letter out, so we can bring it in with us?"

"Certainly, Mr. O'Leary. Here." She popped the latches on the briefcase and extracted the letter, which she handed up from the backseat. He reached back and took it.

"Thanks. Let's go."

They got out of the car, walked the short distance to the Customs office, and went inside. Two uniformed men were sitting behind a counter, chatting with one another. Both looked up as Tim and the others entered, simultaneously asking if they could help.

Business was slow that morning.

Tim spoke first.

"Good morning, gentlemen. This is my wife, Marge O'Leary, and this is my secretary, Madeline Murphy. My name's Tim O'Leary, and I'm an attorney. We're trying to locate Mrs. Murphy's son, who we understand returned to the United States a little over a month ago after an extended absence."

"Do you know where he came in?" said one of the men.

"Right here, apparently. Earlier in the week, we received this letter from Immigration Services, advising us that her son entered the country at the Highwater-North Troy border crossing last month."

Tim handed the letter to him, but he responded without looking at it.

"Hey, we'd love to help," the officer said, "but we don't socialize with the people who come through. We just check their papers, get an idea of where they're heading, and, if they're U.S. citizens, welcome them back home."

Tim had expected something like this, so he had thought of a distinguishing factor that might jog the customs officers' memory.

"Do you get many 'Hannibals' passing through here?"

The two officers looked at one another and laughed.

"Hannibal? Wouldn't that one have had his elephants with him? Nope. Didn't see him."

"Sorry, I'm confusing you. What I meant was the young man's first name is Hannibal. See, it's there in the letter. I thought you'd remember if someone had come through with a name like that."

One of the customs officers, still smiling, replied.

"No offense intended, buddy. It's nice to have a little fun on a slow morning. What's the date of entry on that letter?"

"August twelfth of this year."

"Let's see if we have a copy of the duty roster for that day. Who knows, whoever processed him through might remember. Like you say, that's a real unusual name. Jack, keep an eye on things, while I check in the back, okay?"

"Sure thing, Bert. You folks want a cup of coffee while you wait?"

"Sounds nice, Mr. ... ?"

"Jack's good enough for me. Why don't you and the ladies sit here around the interview table while I get you some coffee."

He set off for the coffee machine behind the counter, as the three of them settled into the folding chairs that flanked three sides of the square table indicated by the customs officer.

Jack returned a few minutes later carrying a tray loaded with cups of coffee, spoons, a milk pitcher, and a small bowl of sugar.

"Compliments of the US government, folks. Your tax dollars at work."

Mrs. Murphy beamed.

"Everything is so pleasant in this state, isn't it? Thank you, Jack."

The others thanked him as well.

"Do you get much traffic through here, Jack?" Tim said.

"Depends. Not much right now, but you'd be surprised how many come and go during the ski season. That will get started by Thanksgiving, and won't be over until April. This Jay Peak is really attracting skiers from Canada."

"They cross the border just for the resort?" said Marge.

"Lots of them. Often for just a day or two, or maybe a week. It's a revolving door. Then in summertime, we get the tourists from the States, who want to see the St. Lawrence River and places like Quebec City, where practically everyone speaks French. Nice people, mostly."

Bert came back, clutching a sheet of paper.

"Hey, Jack, guess who was on duty when their kid came through?"

"How the hell would I know, Bert? Who?"

"Your sister, big guy! She was covering for you for some reason."

"You're kidding. Maggie? She was still a trainee last month. She wasn't even certified yet. That must have been when me and some of the other guys got called out by the fire department down in Lowell, for that big burn up in the mountains. I guess the boss must've cleared her to work during the emergency."

"So, give her a call, why don't you? Maybe she can help these folks."

"Okay. I'll see if she's home. Hold on a minute."

Jack went to the counter, reached over for the phone, dialed a number, and waited.

"Mags? Hey, it's your big brother. How you doing? ... No, nothing's wrong. I'm calling from the office ... Yeah, Customs. No fires today ... The kids are fine ... No, I just have a question. Remember last month when I got called out on that big fire up in the mountains near Lowell, and the boss had you cover for me? ... Right, that one. Well, there's some people here who are looking for a young kid who came over the border one day when you were on duty. They were wondering if you might remember him."

He stopped to listen.

"No, I know we can't remember everyone who comes through. I told them the same thing. But this one's a little different. The kid's name was Hannibal ... I'm not kidding. That was his name—Hannibal. Hannibal Murphy."

He paused again, and then looked surprised.

"You do? You did? No joke. Wait a minute. Let me tell them."

"Hey, folks. My sister remembers him. She gave him a ride."

14

THE MONTH BEFORE, Jack's sister Margaret had looked out the window of the Customs office and seen a young man walking down the road from Canada. He was unshaven and a little disheveled, a sagging backpack on his shoulders. When he arrived at the building, he entered and came over to the counter.

"Is this the United States?" he asked.

"Well, it's not Mexico, buddy," Margaret said. "You've got a couple thousand more miles to go if that's where you're heading."

"No, this is it, at least for now. Sorry, I guess I'm just a little tired. I hitchhiked all night, and my last ride dropped me off in Highwater, almost three miles up the road. I had to walk from there."

He had handed her his passport.

Another surprise.

"Hannibal?"

"That's my name. Strange, isn't it?"

"I guess so. But hey, why am I giving you such a hard time? I'm sorry. You must be exhausted. You sure do look

beat. And wow! Look at these country stamps in your passport. You've been all over the place. Where are you going
from here?"

"Good question. I've been wandering for so long I don't
even know the answer to that myself. Now that you mention
it, I actually started in Mexico after I left the States, and then
went on down through Central America and all over South
America. I was looking for something that I never found."

"That's a long way to go looking for something."

"I finally decided to come back, but I was out of money,
so I got jobs on freighters and cruise ships, one after another,
all the way up the coast, starting in Argentina, and eventually coming down the St. Lawrence to Quebec City. Then I
started hitchhiking. That was a hundred and fifty miles and
almost twenty-four hours ago."

"I'm tired just listening to this!" Margaret said. "How
can I help you?"

"Are there any jobs around here? I'm pretty much tapped
out, moneywise. They let me take some sandwiches when I
got off the ship, but I'll have to buy more food soon."

"Not right around here, I'm afraid. Maybe down at Jay
Peak, though. They'll be starting to gear up for the ski season
soon. Tell you what. Why don't you sit down at the table
over there, and I'll get you something to eat from the back.
We keep juice and coffee cake and things like that, for when
it gets slow and we get hungry. I'm done in less than an hour,
so if you wait around until then, I'll give you a ride to the
resort. It's almost on my way home, and I think you need a
break."

While he waited at the table for Margaret to return, Hanny spotted a pay telephone booth on the other side of the
room. It occurred to him that he should call his mother, with
whom he hadn't had contact in over three years. Then he
realized he had no American coins, so the call would have
to wait.

Margaret returned a few minutes later with a plate full of

crumb cakes and a small container of apple juice. She placed everything on the table in front of Hanny.

"Can I get you some coffee to go with that?"

No, Ma'am, this is fine. Thank you."

"Why don't you call me Margaret? What do people call you? Hannibal?"

"Hanny, mostly. Hannibal is too weird."

He dug into the crumb cakes.

"Okay, Hanny it is. I'll wrap up what I'm doing here, so we can leave as soon as my relief comes in."

Margaret walked back to the desk behind the counter, and sat, making entries in a ledger of some sort, presumably to record Hannibal's entry into the United States.

When her replacement arrived, she gestured toward Hannibal.

"Joe, this is Hannibal Murphy. He's just returned to the States after several years abroad. I'm going to give him a lift down to Jay Peak on my way home. He's hoping to line up a seasonal job there."

"Good for you, kid. They're putting together a real nice resort over there. People are starting to notice. Canadians especially. It's lot easier to get to Jay from where they live than to drive all the way down to Killington for a couple of days' skiing. You a skier?"

"Not me, sir. I'm more of a hiker."

"He sure is, Joe," said Margaret. "He walked all the way down from Highwater last night."

Hanny was a little embarrassed.

"No. I mean hiking on trails, things like that," Hanny said. "In South America. I walked the old Maya, Inca, and Aztec trails when I was trying to learn what had happened to their societies. Their rise and fall, and what they left behind."

"Jay's great for that too, kid. I mean trail hiking, not the other stuff. The Long Trail goes right over the top of the mountain over there. You can hike that section on your day off. A couple of miles almost straight up."

"I'll do that," Hanny said.

"Well, good luck to you. Take care, Mags. See you to-morrow."

"Until then, Joe. C'mon, Hanny. Let's go."

The two of them went out the door and walked around the side of the building to where two cars were parked.

"The green Jeep is mine, Hanny. Hop in on the passenger side and we'll get going."

Margaret opened the door on the driver's side and climbed in behind the wheel. She started the engine as Hanny buckled his seatbelt.

"Ever been in Vermont before, Hanny?"

"No, I haven't. Not until today."

"Well, I think you're going to like it. It's open and wild and free. I've lived here all my life, and I have no intention of leaving. Some day when I get married and start a family, I want it to be here, so this can be theirs too."

"Are you engaged?"

"Oh no, I haven't found the right guy yet. All in good time. There's no rush. I'm only twenty-six. How about you? Got a girl waiting back home?"

"No, too busy wandering around. Besides, I'm a little different from the crowd down in the Bronx where my family lives."

"Well, from what I've seen and heard this morning, you might fit in better with us tree-huggers here in Vermont. Let's head on down to Jay and see what you can find there."

She pulled out of the parking lot and drove south.

15

TIM STOOD and asked Jack for the phone.

"Can I speak to her?"

"Sure thing."

Jack extended the receiver.

"Hello? Margaret? ... Yes, hi. This is Tim O'Leary. I'm here with Madeline Murphy. My wife and I have been trying to help Mrs. Murphy reunite with her son Hannibal, who's been away for a few years. I understand you saw him a month ago?"

He paused, listening.

"Jay Peak? No kidding? That's where we're staying. Is he still there?"

He waited again, then frowned.

"That sounds like it could take some time. Do you know when they'll be back?"

He listened for a few minutes, and asked a few questions. Then he thanked her and handed the phone back to Jack, who said goodbye to his sister and hung up.

Mrs. Murphy didn't know whether to be jubilant at hearing that someone had seen Hanny, or terrified that he had gone missing again. She leaned forward, her face tense. "What happened, Tim? Was there a problem? Is he lost? Did he get hurt?"

"No, he's not hurt. He's just not there. Jack's sister Margaret dropped him off at Jay Peak. Before leaving, she introduced him to a man she knew in the personnel office, telling him what Hanny had been doing these last few years and asking if there were any openings that might be a fit for Hanny. Then she wished Hanny good luck, and went on home. After she left, the man told Hanny they weren't quite ready to staff up for the ski season yet, but, given what Margaret had said about his hiking experience, they had something else that might interest Hanny."

"What was that?" Marge said.

"A special hiking and camping tour was scheduled to go out the next morning, but a problem had developed. One of the guides assigned to the tour had taken a fall while climbing the day before, fracturing his ankle, so he wasn't available. All their other guides had commitments elsewhere, and safety rules threatened cancellation of the tour if a replacement couldn't be found, so they asked Hanny if he'd like to fill in. He accepted, gladly, I imagine. They fitted him out, gave him a bed for the night, and sent him off in the morning with the tour group."

Mrs. Murphy relaxed.

"Oh, that's good. He loves the outdoors, and sitting around a campfire and all that. He'll probably meet some nice people and get to see a little of this pristine area. But that was over a month ago. Shouldn't he be back by now?"

"I guess not. Jack's sister says the trip is a big one. They're going to hike Vermont's Long Trail from Jay Peak down to a place called Sherburne Pass, where the Appalachian Trail splits off to the east. Then they're going to walk the Appalachian Trail all the way to the end, in Maine."

"Maine? How long is this hike?"

"She said altogether it will be over six hundred miles, and

that the last stretch is called the 'Hundred-Mile Wilderness.'"

Mrs. Murphy gasped, collapsing as she did so into a chair. "Six hundred miles? In the woods? Oh, my god. Where will they sleep? What will they eat? Oh, no. Bears, mountain lions, snakes! Oh, my Hanny, my Hanny."

She started to tremble.

Marge tried to console her as Tim continued.

"I don't think so, Mrs. Murphy. Jack's sister said they'd be sleeping in shelters along the trail most nights. Tents the rest of the time. They'll re-provision at stores now and then, and they have experienced professional guides. Don't worry, they'll be okay."

"I hope you're right," Mrs. Murphy said, sniffling.

"It's slow going on the trail," Tim said, "but Hanny will have a great experience. The whole group will be bused back to Jay Peak once they've made it to the end of the trail, at Mount Katahdin in Maine. And he'll get a nice paycheck. Jack's sister thinks they'll be back early next month."

"October?"

"Right. Only a few weeks from now. Why don't we just relax and enjoy our time at the resort. You don't have to go home until Sunday, so that gives you a few more days before flying back to New York."

The three of them thanked Jack and said goodbye, before walking to the parking lot and climbing into Tim's car. As they drove away, Tim had a thought.

"Mrs. Murphy, I think I should get in touch with your brother-in-law Chris. He should be made aware of the fact that Hanny is back in the States. Chris can start to prepare an accounting of what he's done as executor, so I can review it. Then we can wrap things up and get Hanny his inheritance as soon as he returns."

"Oh, would you, Mr. O'Leary? That would be wonderful."

Marge was skeptical.

"What makes you think Chris Murphy will be coopera- tive, Tim? This thing has been his cash cow for several years now. He's not going to give it up easily."

"I know what you're saying, Marge, but as a fiduciary, he's required to account to Hanny. Those are the rules. No exceptions."

"Yes, he has to account to Hanny," Marge said, "but not to you."

"I know," said Tim, "but he's a professional, after all. We can establish that Hanny is back, that he's out of touch temporarily, but will be returning very soon. Chris has to realize that the estate administration should be wound up, and preparations should be made for final distribution. Don't worry."

Marge shrugged, suspecting it wouldn't be as easy as that.

Mrs. Murphy nodded in silent agreement.

16

RATHER THAN STAY through the weekend, Mrs. Murphy decided she would need time to rest up before going back to work on Monday. So, on Friday, Tim and Marge drove her across the state and down to Burlington. Arriving at the airport, they helped her check her suitcase. She kept her plastic bag full of souvenirs and maple syrup she had acquired during the trip. Those she would take with her on the plane.

After wishing her a safe flight, they got back in their car and drove south. An hour later, they arrived at the Trapp Family Lodge in Stowe, Vermont.

The lodge had been established by the iconic Maria von Trapp of *Sound of Music* fame. Baroness Von Trapp had, sadly, died six months ago, but the lodge was still operated by her family. It was situated on 2,500 unspoiled acres in northern Vermont, near the Stowe Mountain ski area, which had been Vermont's first, built during the Great Depression as a Civilian Conservation Corps project.

By the time Tim and Marge reached the lodge, the sun had long since set. Once checked in, they returned to their car and drove a short distance to the small parking area adjacent to the cabin where they would be staying. Stepping out of the car, they looked up. The sky glowed with thousands of stars, shining spectacularly. Tim could not suppress a gasp.

"My lord, Marge, this is stunning! No wonder Chaddie set up his remote observatory in Vermont."

"I remember, Tim. Chadsworth Forester, 'Chaddie.' One of your probate contests, the one with the 'Mystery Will.' That was a wonderful case, and his Foundation's work still goes on down on Long Island, but this is the place to be if you want to gaze at the stars. And I don't mean with a telescope." She took his hand in hers, and they walked up the steps to their cabin.

As they entered, they saw two cozy chairs in front of a wood burning fireplace, already stacked with kindling and firewood and ready to go. A four-poster bed with brightly colored pillows and bedspread beckoned.

"Tim, let's light the fire and climb into that bed. It looks so inviting. We can try the chairs later."

Tim did as he was told, while Marge pulled back the bedspread and propped up the pillows so they could watch the fire from the bed.

"Oh, Tim, this is our second honeymoon, isn't it?"

"Almost better than the first, Marge, if that's possible."

And then they spoke no further, letting their bodies communicate for them. It was twenty minutes before they looked at each other, smiled, and sat up to look at the fire, which was still burning brightly.

"So, what should we do for an encore, Marge?"

"Well, there's always a repeat performance, but let's make some plans for tomorrow first."

"Fair enough. How about the Saturday night 'Austrian Dance Festival' they were promoting back in the lobby when we checked in?"

"I saw that sign too. It sounds wonderful. I haven't done a waltz since high school dance class. So romantic. Strauss, The Blue Danube Waltz. The Vienna Waltz. Oh, I love this place!"

* * *

They hiked the Lodge's trails the next day, climbing to the top of the mountain, then down to an old stone chapel. They peeked into a sugar house, dormant until spring, when the sap would start running. They looked for, but never found, a still they believed must be making moonshine somewhere in these hills, and generally had an exhilarating but exhausting time. By mid-afternoon they were ready for a nap, so they headed back to their cabin to get a little rest before the evening's Austrian Dance Festival. They tumbled into the bed, with enough energy to make love again before falling fast asleep.

* * *

"Tim, wake up! We're going to be late."

He rolled over and looked at the bedside clock, which registered 5:45 p.m. The dance festival would start in forty-five minutes.

A quick shower, shared "to save time." Then they dressed, and walked toward the main building, where a tent had been set up on the meadow. Tables were arranged under the tent, one end of which was open, with a temporary dance floor on the lawn outside. In the background, the mountains glowed in the setting sun. A small group of musicians, wearing colorfully decorated leather shorts, white shirts, leather vests, and black, feathered hats, was warming up next to the dance floor.

"Shouldn't they be dressed in tuxedos?" Marge said.

"I think so. Maybe they're going for a country flavor."

"They don't have violins either. One of them even has a guitar, and that one has an accordion. Hey, there's a guy standing at a table, hitting a paddle with a stick and fooling around with a bell. What in the world?"

Just then, one of the musicians grabbed the microphone. He tipped his black felt hat.

"Herzlich willkommen, meine damen und herren. Welcome!" he shouted, to enthusiastic applause. "Welcome, ladies and gentlemen. We will be entertaining you this evening with the music of our homeland, a land of mountains and streams, beautiful skies, a land like this one. Now take your seats and let us show you how we dance while you enjoy your dinner. Then you will join us on the dance floor, and we will all celebrate our countries together."

He spun around to face his band mates.

"Meine freunde! Ein schuhplattler, wurdest du bitte!"

The band roared into action, and eight dancers, similarly attired but with leather suspenders rather than vests, skipped out onto the dance floor and began hopping from foot to foot, clapping their hands, and alternately slapping their thighs and the soles of their feet in time to the music. The crowd roared its approval.

"I don't think this is a waltz, Tim."

"I think you're right, Marge." He started to laugh. "Might as well enjoy it. Let's sit down."

They found a table with a couple of empty seats, as the band played on and the crowd clapped in time with the dancers. When the music stopped for a moment, they introduced themselves to the others at their table.

"Hi, I'm Marge O'Leary and this is my husband Tim."

"Hi, Marge, Tim. We're the Schusters, Karl and Karen, and these two are our friends, the Nichols, Jim and Muriel."

"Nice to meet you guys. Do you know when the waltzes will start?"

"The waltzes?"

"Yes, the waltzes. Strauss, the Blue Danube, the Austrian music."

"This is the Austrian music. They just did the Schuhplattler. It's a folk dance. Then they'll do others. There won't be any waltzes tonight."

"So that's why they're not wearing tuxedos and playing violins?"

"Right, this is Austrian folk music. Those are the instruments they use, and the clothes they wear. Lederhosen."

"Lay their hose and? And what?"

"Lederhosen. Leather pants. It's traditional. Soon the leader will ask all of us to join in. It's really a lot of fun."

Marge looked at her husband.

"Good you didn't rent a tuxedo, Tim."

"And you were wishing you had brought your old prom dress."

"What shall we do?

"A shoe platter, I guess. Looks hard, though."

Karl Schuster laughed.

"Not after a few glasses of schnapps, it isn't. Hey, waiter!"

17

BY WEDNESDAY, Tim was back in the office, and anxious to contact Mrs. Murphy's brother-in-law to discuss the winding up of her ex-husband's estate. Now that her son had been found, it was time to close the estate account and distribute the assets to Hannibal, who could then use them as he saw fit. In particular, of course, he could rely on them for his own support and financial well-being, as he moved on to the next phase of his life.

Tim called Mrs. Murphy into his office.

"Yes, Mr. O'Leary?"

"Do you have your brother-in-law's phone number?" he said. "I think I should give him a call and let him know we've located Hanny. It's time for him to account for his administration of your late husband's estate. Then he can distribute the estate assets to Hanny, so Hanny can select an investment advisor to manage them for him. I'm assuming the assets are in interest-bearing bank accounts now, but probably should be more diversified for the long run. Your son will need guidance to accomplish that."

"Oh, yes, certainly, Mr. O'Leary. Please do call Chris. He

doesn't speak to me, so it would be wonderful if you made the call."

"I will. Now did Hanny give you his power of attorney?"

"No, I'm afraid not. Mrs. O'Leary asked me the same question. All I have is that form you used to find out which countries Hanny visited. The one that made me some kind of 'credited representative.'"

"All right. I'll call Chris and let him know Hanny is back in the States and should be home in a few weeks. Hopefully, he'll be cooperative, as a matter of professional courtesy."

"Your lips to God's ears, Mr. O'Leary. Your lips to God's ears."

She crossed herself as she rose, not an encouraging sign.

"I'll be right back with his phone number."

Tim reached for the telephone as she returned and handed him a business card. He dialed the number on the card and waited.

"Christopher Murphy's office. May I help you?"

"Yes, thank you. This is Tim O'Leary calling Mr. Murphy."

"May I ask what this is about?"

"Yes, I'm an attorney, and I'm calling about the estate of Mr. Murphy's brother, Francis. Madeline Murphy is my secretary. She's asked me to speak to Mr. Murphy with regard to her son Hannibal's interest in his father's estate."

"Hold on, please."

A moment later, another voice came on the phone.

"What does she want this time!"

"Excuse me? Is this Mr. Murphy?"

"Yes, it is. What does my former sister-in-law want now? I told her a thousand times I'm not spending my brother's assets chasing down her loony son."

"Mr. Murphy, I don't think language like that is necessary."

"Well, get to it, then."

"It's my understanding that her son is the sole beneficiary of your late brother's estate, and as to chasing him down, that won't be necessary. He returned to the United States last month."

'You don't say. Where?"

"He's currently working with an environmental tour company in New England. As soon as he completes his current assignment, I expect he'll be back here in New York and ready to take distribution of his inheritance. I thought I should apprise you of his return so you could put together your accounting for his review, and then we can wind up the estate."

"Are you saying you're his attorney?"

"No. As I mentioned to your secretary when she answered the phone, Hannibal's mother works for me. She asked me to call you to let you know he's back, and to start the process for distributing the estate assets to him."

"Well, when you see him, tell him his uncle has serious questions about his competence, and will not distribute anything to him without a court order. Goodbye."

He slammed down the phone.

Tim was stunned. It was a few seconds before he recovered sufficiently to return his own phone to its cradle. Looking up, he saw that Mrs. Murphy was standing at the door to his office, nervously touching her gray-streaked hair.

"I could hear him shouting, Mr. O'Leary. I'm so sorry to have subjected you to that. Chris can be terribly nasty at times. Maybe we should just forget about this."

"We can't do that, Mrs. Murphy. Hannibal is entitled to receive his inheritance. Your brother-in-law knows that, but it sounds like he's going to do whatever he can to prevent it from happening. I don't know if it's the commissions, the fees, or something else entirely, but it's pretty clear that he'll be putting up roadblocks every step of the way. He even suggested that your son is incompetent, which makes me think he might try to argue that Hanny should have a court-appointed guardian, presumably Chris himself, to handle the funds. One way or the other, he's obviously determined to hang onto the estate."

"But Hanny's not incompetent. Just because he's different

doesn't mean he's incompetent."

"I know that, and your brother-in-law presumably does as well. It's probably something he thought up on the spur of the moment. By the way, do you have a copy of Frank's Will?"

"Yes, I do. I keep it in a file with Hanny's other papers. Would you like to see it?"

"Please."

"I have it at home. I used to keep his papers here, but I took them with me when we went to Vermont to look for him. I didn't bring them back here afterwards. I'll get the file and the copy of Frank's Will tonight and bring them with me tomorrow."

"Good. Thanks."

18

"THAT CHRIS MURPHY is a piece of work."

"Chris Murphy?" Marge said.

"Yeah. Mrs. Murphy's former brother-in-law. Frank's brother. He's the executor of Frank's estate."

"What's going on?"

"I called him today to let him know that Hanny is back, figuring he'd be happy to learn that he can finally wind up the estate and turn over the assets."

"And he wasn't?"

"To say the least. He practically bit my head off, told me to get lost, then hung up on me."

"He doesn't really have a choice, does he? Hanny is the beneficiary."

"I know, Marge, but I think he might try to dream something up to prevent it from happening."

"Like what?"

"Like saying Hanny's incompetent and needs a guardian to handle his money for him."

"And the guardian would be?"

"I think he has himself in mind. He'd conjure up something about Mrs. Murphy being bad with money, incapable of managing a fund of this size, etcetera, etcetera."

"But Tim, if he feels that way about Mrs. Murphy and Hanny, would a judge subject the two of them to having him in control of Hanny's assets, even if he has done a good job managing his brother's estate? Assuming he has, of course."

"I don't think so. I think he hatched that scenario on the fly. His reaction was so extreme that I can't help thinking there's something more to this. Something having to do with his brother's estate and his own handling of it."

"How would you be able to find out about that?"

"I can't, at least not unless Hanny retains me as his attorney. Then I could approach his uncle again and ask him to tell me what I need to know if I'm going to advise Hanny about his interest in the estate."

"And if he still resists?"

"Hanny would have to authorize me to bring what's known as a compulsory accounting proceeding in the Bronx County Surrogate's Court."

"The Bronx? Why there?"

"Hanny's father lived in Riverdale, in the Bronx, when he died. So that's where his Will was probated."

"Too bad you won't be able to talk to Hanny for a while, not unless you want to hunt for him in the Maine woods."

"I think I'll pass on that."

"Oh, by the way, not to change the subject, but the Livingstons invited us to the ballet at Lincoln Center on Saturday."

"The ballet? I'm not sure I'd like that. Can't we tell them we have something else scheduled for that night?"

"Tim! You know we don't. Besides, it's a matinee."

"Then we could say we have to go to a funeral on Saturday."

"Are you trying to be funny? Anyway, I already told Sue we'd love to go."

19

AS PROMISED, MRS. MURPHY ARRIVED in the office the following day carrying a folder stuffed with papers. They included
a copy of her late husband Francis' Will, which she placed
on Tim's desk, before returning to her own. She was on the
phone when he came in a few minutes later. Covering the
mouthpiece with one hand, she whispered:

"Frank's Will is on your desk, Mr. O'Leary," she whispered, covering the mouthpiece with one hand.

Tim saw the Will, and picked it up. Reading it, he saw
that, while Hanny was in fact the sole beneficiary, his receipt
of the estate funds was to be postponed until he reached the
age of twenty-five. In the meantime, the estate was to be held
in trust. Surprisingly, the trustee was none other than Madeline Murphy.

"Mrs. Murphy, would you come in here, please?"

She appeared at the door to his office, pen and notepad
in hand.

"Yes, Mr. O'Leary."

"Mrs. Murphy, you didn't tell me you were the trustee
under Frank's Will."

"The what?"

"The trustee. Of the trust for your son."

"I didn't know there was a trust for Hanny. I thought he was the beneficiary of the estate."

"Well, he is. But since your husband died prematurely, and Hanny was still young, the estate was to be held in trust for him until he reached age twenty-five, and you're the trustee of the trust. Didn't anyone tell you that?"

"I don't think so. Isn't Chris the executor?"

"Yes, but a trustee is different from an executor. An executor probates the Will, collects the estate assets, pays the debts, the taxes and the estate expenses, and then distributes what's left to the beneficiaries. In this case the trust for your son is the sole beneficiary, unless he's already twenty-five. Then there's no trust, and it all goes to him outright. How old is Hanny, anyway?"

"He'll be twenty-five on his next birthday."

"And you didn't know you were the trustee?"

"No. I mean it was all so upsetting. Hanny out of touch for almost a year. Chris being so nasty about everything. I just did what I was told, and tried to put it all out of my mind."

"Did what you were told?"

"Yes. You know, signing papers and things like that."

"What did you sign?"

"I don't know. Papers. Whatever Chris wanted me to sign."

"Do you have copies?"

"I guess. Everything is in the same file that copy of the Will was in. Why, is it important?"

"It could be. Could you show me the file?"

Mrs. Murphy hustled out, and was back in less than a minute.

"Here it is."

Tim opened the file and leafed through the papers inside. Most had to do with the probate proceeding, or the lawsuit against the driver of the car involved in the accident that killed Francis Murphy. One, however, was a surprise.

"Mrs. Murphy, this is what they call a certificate of letters of trusteeship," Tim said. "It shows that the court formally appointed you as trustee of the trust set up for Hanny under Frank's Will, so what the Will said was confirmed in writing by the court. Did you know that?"

"Well, Chris might have said something about a trust, and me being a trustee, but I couldn't make heads or tails of it. He said it would require him to do more work, for which he would have to charge, of course. And he said it was stupid, because nothing was in the trust, anyway, so I shouldn't worry about having to actually do anything."

"That isn't surprising, but what confuses me is why your ex-husband would make you the trustee of a trust for Hanny. He named his brother Chris as his executor. Why not name Chris as Hanny's trustee?"

"I don't know, Mr. O'Leary. Maybe it was because he knew his brother didn't think much of Hanny. I'm Hanny's mother, and Frank knew how much I loved my son, so I guess he thought I was the one who'd take good care of him. Is that what a trustee does?"

"Yes. That's what a trustee does, Mrs. Murphy, and now you're going to take good care of Hanny by making his uncle turn over Frank's property to you."

"He won't want to do that, Mr. O'Leary."

"No, but we're going to make him. Sit down. I want you to type something up for me."

20

TIM FELT A BIT NOSTALGIC as he turned right off Columbus Avenue and drove west on 62nd Street toward the Lincoln Center parking garage. Fordham Law School stood to his left, on the south side of the street, and he realized he hadn't been back since he walked away from the school after his last exam almost twenty years earlier. He decided he'd like to return for his twentieth reunion, now less than a year away.

"Here it is, Tim!" Marge was pointing to the garage entrance just ahead on the right. "This is going to be great."

They drove down the ramp and into the underground garage, parked the car, and got out. After finding the elevator and riding it back to ground level, they walked outside to the main plaza, and looked around at the impressive facades of the surrounding theaters.

"I can't believe I never climbed the steps to see any of this when I was in law school," Tim said. "I studied right around the corner for three years, and the closest I ever came was when I'd walk along that sidewalk over there to get to the subway station up on 66th Street."

"Well, here we are now," Marge said, breaking into a

broad smile as she admired the striking architecture. "I wonder where the Livingstons are. Oh, wait, there!"

"Sue! Charlie! Over here!" She pulled Tim by the arm and ran toward the fountain, as their friends saw them and waved.

"Hey, guys," said Sue. "Ready to soak up some culture, Tim?"

"I'll do my best, Sue. Charlie, have you been to the ballet before?"

"Only the time my parents forced me to go to my little sister's recital. That was thirty years ago. I wanted to go to a baseball game, or something fun like that, but you know how parents are. Off we went. In the end, I must admit, it was sort of cute, and it was nice to see how happy it made my sister that we were all there. That was it, though. I did my time. I've been able to duck it since then."

"So, what happened today? Did your luck ran out?" Marge said.

"Sue tricked me, pure and simple," Charlie said, rolling his eyes. "She told me she had a surprise for our anniversary, and that it would be in Lincoln Center in the 'Big Apple.' I thought she meant the Big Apple Circus. I know the circus is in Lincoln Center, and that's where she said we were going. but what I didn't know was that the circus doesn't start until Christmastime. She guarantees I'll like it. Right, Sue?"

"Yes, I do, buddy boy, I guarantee it. You'll probably be begging me to get season tickets after today."

Charlie looked at Tim and shrugged his shoulders.

"If you insist, dear. Now where is this thing, anyway?"

"Right over there." Sue indicated the New York State Theater. "The ballet starts in twenty minutes. We'd better get started. We have some climbing to do. We're in the fifth ring."

Tim was confused. "The fifth ring? What's that?"

"You can tell from here that the theater is really big," she said, "and see how tall it is? The best seats are on the main level, but we were pretty late ordering our tickets, and the best we could do was the fifth ring. It's on the sides of the fourth ring, which is the highest balcony."

"Hope no one here is afraid of heights," Charlie said.

"The dancers will look like dolls," said Sue, "but the acoustics are fabulous. Come on, let's go."

Once inside, Sue recommended taking the stairs. She said it would be a chore, but that the wait for the elevators made sense only for the handicapped, so the stairs were the way to go.

Charlie couldn't resist. "But Sue, Tim has a handicap. A big one."

She blanched.

"Tim? I didn't know that. Are you okay with the stairs?"

"Don't pay attention to him, Sue. He's making fun of my golf game."

"Oh, I get it. Okay, up we go."

The four of them climbed the stairs, which, as predicted, seemed endless, until they finally reached the highest balcony. They found their seats far to the right. Surprisingly, there were no seats in front of them. Or behind them, for that matter. Tim wouldn't have been surprised if oxygen masks fell down from above. Theatergoers having a fear of heights need not apply. Surprisingly, though, the view of the stage was quite good, as was the view of the orchestra, which was already warming up.

Tim braced himself for a long afternoon.

Then the music started.

Far below, a girl, seemingly the size of a pixie, floated onto the stage on her toes, spreading her arms as she turned in weightless circles, not so much in time with the music, as a part of it. Then there were three, then five, the music flowing through them, and to them, as Tim sat transfixed. Could it be that this would be something he would actually enjoy?

Sue leaned across Marge and offered him her opera glasses. Tim declined with a polite wave of his hand. He knew nothing could improve on what he was seeing. Reality could never match fantasy.

Nearly an hour later, Sue and Marge took advantage of a fifteen minute intermission to use the ladies' room. Neither of them spoke, and Marge almost tiptoed past Charlie, who seemed to have nodded off. They returned just in time for the second act, whispering about how long the line had been. Tim started to say something to Marge about the first act, but she put her finger to her lips, pointing to the still snoozing Charlie. Then the second act began, and Tim quickly found himself entranced once more. Awareness of time was suspended, as dreamy detachment prevailed.

The performance ended an hour later, and Tim rose to applaud, startling Marge, to say nothing of. Charlie, who had apparently woken up, only to nod off again. Sue, however, was not surprised. She also rose, and turning to Tim, said, "I could see it happening, Tim. You loved it, didn't you."

"I did. I really did. I never thought I would, but I did. It was like a fantasy, playing out on a stage somewhere far below us." He kept clapping, as did Marge and Sue. Charlie, now awake, figured he'd better join in, so he began to clap as well, although a bit half-heartedly.

They descended the stairs and went outside, where they said their goodbyes. Marge was delighted that Tim was taken with the performance. Sue scolded Charlie for falling asleep. Charlie said Tim was just being polite, but, without prompting, Tim summed up the experience.

"It was like we were in the heavens, looking down on the beautiful side of life, a side I rarely see from the perspective of my profession. I went to a baroque concert up at the Cathedral of Saint John the Divine many years ago, and at first, I loved the music and the setting. But as it wore along and became repetitive, and the wooden seats became so uncomfortable, it turned into a torture, and I decided that sophisticated art wasn't for me. It wasn't something I could appreciate, so I've avoided it ever since, but now I want to make up for

lost time. Let's do it again. Maybe something else next time.
Maybe the Philharmonic."

Sue thought that was a splendid idea. "Yes, let's. Marge,
I'll give you a call. Don't look so sad, Charlie. You can still
go to a Yankees game once in a while."

21

ON MONDAY, WITH MRS. MURPHY'S PERMISSION, Tim called Chris Murphy's office. The secretary put him through, and Murphy came on the line.

"Didn't I tell you not to bother me anymore? You don't even have a client. Keep this up and I'll file a complaint with the Bar Association. Now go away, or—"

Tim cut him off.

"I do have a client, Mr. Murphy. Hannibal's mother has retained me to represent her."

"Her? She has no interest in Frank's estate. She gave that up when she divorced him. You should know that. Now get lost, or so help me, God—"

"Mr. Murphy, I think you'd better stop this. You know very well that Hannibal's interest in his father's estate is to be held in trust until he's twenty-five, and the trustee is my client, Mrs. Murphy."

Silence.

"Where'd you get that information?"

"From your brother's Will, which I have now seen, and from the certificate issued by the court confirming her appointment as trustee."

"Oh, aren't you the smart one. Well, maybe you should have done the rest of your homework. That kid must be twenty-five by now, so that makes him the beneficiary, not that stupid trust. Why my brother ever appointed his dingbat ex to be a trustee, I'll never know. Thank heaven she won't get to play that role now. So, bug off, will you? I'm holding everything here until I hear from the kid, and then I'll have the court appoint me as the guardian of his property, so he won't blow it on some harebrained expedition to find Conan Doyle's *Lost World*."

"But he isn't twenty-five yet. He's only twenty-four."

"Well, then, he won't have to wait long. I'll get that petition for my appointment as his guardian ready. Then I can give it to him as his birthday present. Now, are we done here?"

"No, we're not. I called as a courtesy, to tell you was that I filed a petition in the Bronx County Surrogate's Court on Friday afternoon. My client is seeking to compel you to account to her, as trustee of her son's trust, for your administration of your brother's estate."

"Oh, really. They'll make short work of that trash. Assuming they get around to reading it before the new year. They won't even have a judge over there until then."

"The clerk issues citations, not the judge, and, because of the urgency of the situation, a citation has already been issued, directing you to show cause why you should not be compelled to account. The citation, and a copy of the petition, will be served on you today, unless you agree to appear voluntarily, and file your notice of appearance with the court. The citation is returnable a week from Friday. May I assume you'll appear without my having to serve you?"

"Assume nothing, O'Leary. Do whatever you feel like doing."

"I figured that. I'll let you go. Someone may be waiting to see you."

Tim was hanging up when he heard the other man shout, "Who the hell are you?"

His process server had apparently arrived in Murphy's office.

22

MRS. MURPHY HAD BEEN INVITED by Tim to sit across from him when he called her brother-in-law, in case he might need to ask her any questions during the call. She looked pained when he put down the phone.

"What did he say? You sounded annoyed. Did he refuse to cooperate?"

"He did, but he doesn't have a choice. I think my process server just arrived in his office with the papers. He'll have to be in court a week from Friday, or he could be in serious trouble. And assuming he does show up, the judge will give him a deadline to submit a detailed accounting of what he's done with his brother's estate."

"Does Hanny have to be there?"

"No, I'll appear on your behalf. That's all that's necessary for now, but it might be nice if we could find Hanny before then. He's going to be twenty-five pretty soon, and then he'll have to be involved because his trust will disappear, for all intents and purposes."

"Disappear?"

"Yes. The estate will be payable directly to him at that

point. It won't go through the trust. Hanny will need to get
personally involved, whether he likes it or not."

Mrs. Murphy was uncharacteristically firm.

"Then we'll find him. I'm going up there."

"Going up where?

"To that trail he's walking on, the one called the Appli-
ance Trail."

"You mean the Appalachian Trail?"

"Whatever. I'm going up there and tell him he's got to
come home."

"I don't think that's such a good idea, Mrs. Murphy.
That's rugged country. Have you ever hiked in the mountains? In the woods?"

"Not even a girl scout camping trip, Mr. O'Leary, but I'm
going."

Tim was shocked. Was this really Mrs. Murphy, or had
her double shown up this morning? He thought it best to
reason with her, or at least to slow her down.

"Let's think this through, Mrs. Murphy. There must be a
better way. Give me some time. I'll come up with something.
Just give me some time."

"How much time?"

"Let me sleep on it. I'll talk to Marge tonight. She might
have some thoughts or suggestions. Then you and I can make
some decisions tomorrow."

"I've already made my decision."

"I know, but give me until tomorrow."

"Tomorrow." She stood and walked out of the room.

* * *

"She wants to what?"

"She wants to go up to Maine and find her son."

"He's hiking on the Appalachian Trail. That's practically
in the wilderness. Is she going in her high heels?"

"I know. I know. I think this thing with her brother-in-
law has finally driven her over the edge."

"Well, there's no way she can do that. No way. She'll have to listen to reason."

"She's determined, Marge. I've never seen her like this. I think she'll go. High heels or not."

"She can't, Tim. We have to stop her."

"I don't know if we can. You wouldn't believe how firm she was. It was a different Mrs. Murphy than the one we've come to know."

"Well, she can't go alone. Someone would have to go with her."

"I agree, but who, and even if there was such a person, Mrs. Murphy wouldn't last an hour on the trail. She obviously doesn't realize how rugged those things are. There has to be a way to intercept her son without trying to chase him down in the woods."

"Doesn't it cross roads?"

"I guess. Otherwise, it would have to tunnel under them. We crossed a few when were up at the Trapp Lodge last week. They weren't big, though. Why, what are you thinking?"

"You could drive up there with her, and wait at a crossing near a town along the route. Maybe stay in a motel the night before they're supposed to come through."

"But how do we know where they'll be at any particular time on any particular day?"

"They must have a schedule. Why don't you call the resort up at Jay Peak? They should be able to help."

She pointed to one of the brochures from their stay at Jay, which was sitting on the counter. Tim picked it up, flipped through it, and found the resort's phone number. He reached for the wall phone, took the handset off its cradle, and dialed the resort.

"Hi! My name's Tim O'Leary. My wife and I stayed with you recently, and a friend's son joined one of your hikes shortly before we got there. I'd like to speak to someone in the department that handles those things ... Thanks."

Tim held the handset away from his ear.

"They're transferring me to their 'Adventure Team.'"

Someone came on the line.

"Yes? You are? ... Thanks, no, I'm not looking to book a camping expedition. I'm just checking to see where one that went out last month would be right now. It started on August thirteenth and was going all the way to Mount Katahdin in Maine ... Yes, that's right, the Long Trail and then the Appalachian Trail ... They did? Well, do you know when they'll arrive? ... Okay ... Yes, I will. Thank you. Good night."

He hung up.

"What did they say, Tim?"

"He said they're almost finished, but that the last stretch is the toughest. It's called the Hundred Mile Wilderness. That's where they are now. They should be at Mount Katahdin and the end of the trail by tomorrow afternoon. Until then, they'll be out of radio contact. He also said that once they reach Mount Katahdin, which is in Baxter State Park, they'll come down to park headquarters, and then be shuttled to a motel in a little town called Millinocket for a celebration dinner and a night's rest. The day after tomorrow, they'll board a charter bus and be driven back to Jay Peak."

"So, what do you think?"

"I'll try to convince Mrs. Murphy to sit tight for a day or so. Then she can call the office at Jay Peak and see if they can get Hanny on the phone. Maybe if she's able to talk to him, she'll calm down."

"And if she doesn't?"

SHE DIDN'T.

"I don't care, Mr. O'Leary. I'm not taking a chance. I know Hanny. He might fall in love with that "Wilderness" you're talking about, and turn around and walk back into it when his group is dropped off at the motel for their celebration. Like I said, I'm not taking any chances. I want to go up there, and be there when they bring him down from the mountain."

"But, Mrs. Murphy, they'll be at the end of the trail this afternoon, and in the motel nearby tonight. First thing tomorrow morning, they'll be getting on a bus and driving back to Jay Peak. If you really insist on going, why not go to Jay, and greet Hanny when he gets off the bus tomorrow? He's not going to walk away from the group without getting paid, and that won't happen until they're back at the resort."

"How do you know that, Mr. O'Leary?"

"Well, I don't, but it stands to reason, doesn't it? They're not going to reach out the bus window and hand him a pay envelope, as they head off to Jay and he walks back into the woods."

"They could hand him a check, couldn't they?"

"But he'd have to cash it, wouldn't he?"

"He might do that at a local bank. I'm sorry, but I'm worried. Hanny is very resourceful. I want to go today."

"Mrs. O'Leary, I can't take you up there today. I have a conference this morning, and the drive is probably eight or nine hours, even with only a couple of stops for gas and food. That means we'd get there very late tonight."

"I can drive myself. I didn't say you had to come. I can leave now. I'll just call the temp agency, so they can send someone over."

"I couldn't let you do that. You've told me you're not used to driving on the interstate. You said it scares you. I ..."

He sighed and shrugged his shoulders.

"All right, I give up. Go next door and ask the travel agent if there are any flights going up there this afternoon. If there are, get two tickets. I'll go with you. It might be a good idea for me to meet Hanny, anyway, if I'm going to be working with him on his father's estate."

"Oh, thank you, Mr. O'Leary. Thank you. I'll be right back. You don't have to pay me for today. Or for tomorrow, of course."

"Don't worry about that. Just go."

She hurried out the door. Twenty minutes later, she was back, frowning and fighting back tears.

"The travel agent says no one flies to that town, that Millinocket. The closest they go is a city in Maine called Bangor."

"How far is it from Millinocket?"

"Mrs. Tandy, she's the travel agent, she said it's seventy-five miles away."

"Don't they have rental cars at the airport?"

Mrs. Murphy brightened.

"I didn't think of that. How stupid of me. I'll ask."

Ten minutes later, she was back again.

"They do! And Mrs. Tandy also had another idea."

"What?"

"She said there's a charter service that could fly us right from Bangor to a little airport in Millinocket. It's called 'On Eagles Wings,' and she knows the owner. She could get us a good price. Oh, and of course, I'll pay for all of this."

"Well, that's very nice of you, but why do we need to do that? Renting a car and driving up there would only take a couple of hours."

"Oh, of course. I'll go back and get the plane tickets. There's a nonstop flight from LaGuardia this afternoon at 2:25. It gets to Bangor a little after four."

"Fine. I'll call Marge and tell her we're going."

"Thank you, thank you, thank you. I'm going to see Hanny at last. I can't believe it. Thank you."

She couldn't stop smiling as she practically skipped out of his office. Tim picked up the phone and called home.

"Hey, hon. Guess who's going to Maine? ... No, I couldn't talk her out of it. It turns out you can fly up there, or at least part of the way. I think I'd better go with her, just in case she needs help, plus I can finally meet her son and talk to him. I'll see if I can convince him to come home. That way he can be at the courthouse when the compulsory accounting proceeding goes before the surrogate. I'll have to stay overnight, but I'll be home tomorrow."

He listened for a few seconds.

"No, this is a regular airline. There's some small plane charter service that can take us the last seventy-five miles from the Bangor airport, but small planes make me nervous. I told Mrs. Murphy I'd rather get a rental car. That way, I can also drive both of them home after we fetch Hanny."

He paused again.

"Don't worry. I'll be careful. Tell the kids I'll bring them a present from Maine. I'll call you when we get up there tonight. Bye. Love you."

He hung up the phone.

Mrs. Murphy was back in a few minutes.

"All set! Mrs. Tandy said we can pay for the plane tickets

at the airport. May I go home and pack?"

Tim realized he didn't even have a toothbrush. Well, no time to go home now. His conference started in less than an hour. He'd just have to hope he could pick up a few things in Millinocket when they got there.

"Go ahead. Just tell Mrs. Turner to activate the answering machine before she leaves today."

— 24 —

THE FLIGHT TO BANGOR was smooth and short. Mrs. Murphy had insisted on paying for the tickets. She sat in the window seat, hoping she could catch a glimpse of Mount Katahdin, where Hanny should have been right about then. The fact that the mountain would never be closer than seventy-five miles from their approach to Bangor airport did nothing to dampen her enthusiasm for what she referred to as "an unforgettable shared experience."

They landed on time in Bangor in the late afternoon. Tim walked straight to the rental car counter in the baggage claim area, while Mrs. Murphy waited for her suitcase. A pleasant young rental agent greeted him with a smile, and asked how she could help.

He handed her his driver's license.

"I need a car that will seat three and a modest amount of luggage. We'll be driving to Millinocket this afternoon and staying overnight. Tomorrow, we'll drive back to New York and drop the car off there."

The agent, whose name plate identified her as Wendy, frowned.

"Oh, I'm sorry, you won't be able to get to Millinocket today. There's been an accident on the Main Street causeway, at the crossing between Dolby Pond and the Partridge Brook Flowage. Route 11 is closed and we're told they won't be able to clear the wreckage and reopen the causeway until sometime tomorrow morning."

"But we wanted to get there today."

"I'm so sorry. Is it urgent?"

"In a way, yes."

"Well, I suppose you could consider On Eagles Wings. They could fly you up to Millinocket Municipal Airport. Barry lives in Millinocket, and he usually flies his Cessna back there at the end of the day. He might be willing to take you along. You'd have to pay him, of course."

"I've heard of that company. There are two of us. Will we both fit?"

"Of course. His Cessna seats four people, including the pilot."

Tim hesitated.

"Are those things safe?"

"Oh, certainly. His office is right over there, on the other side of the terminal. You can practically see it from here. Why don't you get your luggage and walk over? I'll call Barry and tell him you're coming."

"Uh, thanks, I guess I'm a little nervous about small planes, Wendy. May I call you that?"

"You certainly may. I'm sorry I couldn't help you with the car. We have a small office in Millinocket. If you'd like, I'll call up there now and tell them to have a car ready for you when you arrive. The office will be closed by then, but they'll leave a car out front, with a key in the ignition."

"They'd do that? Couldn't it be stolen?"

She glanced at his driver's license and smiled. "We're honest people up here, Mr. O'Leary. The car will be waiting for you. You can sign the rental agreement tomorrow. Now you'd better get moving. Barry might sneak out early if he's having a quiet day."

Walking toward the baggage carousel, Tim saw Mrs. Murphy extricating her large suitcase from the line of bags rolling along the belt. She was not a small woman, but the bag seemed to be fighting back.

"Let me help you with that, Mrs. Murphy."

Tim reached around her and grabbed the suitcase by the handle. It didn't budge.

"Whoa! I forgot how heavy this was when we checked it in New York. This much for one night?"

"I packed some things for Hanny. You told me the customs officer said all he had was a little backpack when he crossed the border. And it's getting chilly up here."

"Some things? This feels like you cleaned out the Orvis store back home. Anyway, we've got a little problem."

"What problem?"

"There's been a crash on the road to Millinocket. The road's closed until tomorrow."

"But Hanny's leaving tomorrow. Even if he doesn't turn around and walk back into the woods, he'll be in a bus on his way to Vermont."

"I know, but do you remember what that travel agent told you about the air charter service? On Eagles Wings?"

"Yes, but you said we weren't going to use it."

"Well, maybe we will. The desk clerk at the car rental agency said the man who runs it is here, and that he's flying up to Millinocket this afternoon. She's going to call him to see if he can take us."

"Oh, please, God. My head is spinning. We're so close. How will we find out?"

"We're going to walk over to see him right now. That is, if I don't have a heart attack trying to carry your bag."

They walked toward the far side of the terminal, as instructed by Wendy, and before long spotted the On Eagles Wings sign on a wall behind a counter. Approaching it, they caught the attention of a bearded young man fussing with some paperwork, and getting ready to close up for the day. He looked up as he noticed them.

"You must be the people who're looking for a ride to Millinocket."

"That's us," Tim said, smiling. "You must be Barry. Can you take us?"

"I can indeed. I'll be done here in a couple of minutes. Then I'll take you out to the plane. The fare will be seventy-five dollars each. No charge for the luggage, unless of course it's over fifty pounds."

"Afraid so, Barry. It feels like it weighs a ton."

"Okay, but then I have to put it in one of the passenger seats and strap it in, so the plane's load is balanced. It's a small plane, you know. There's also the added fuel consumption. Sorry, but I'll have to charge you for the suitcase. Let's say fifty dollars. Will that be all right?"

"Sure, Barry. Can you take a credit card?"

"Not a problem. Give me the card. I'll run the charge, and then we can get going."

— 25 —

BARRY'S PLANE was a small, single-engine Cessna. Before boarding, he asked Tim and Mrs. Murphy how much they weighed, and then he personally weighed the suitcase. He told them he needed to balance the plane's load to achieve optimum stability in the air. He also demonstrated evacuation procedures in the event of a forced landing, and showed them a little bag which contained survival essentials should there be one. He said he was required to do all this, but they should not be concerned. It would be, he said, laughing, basically the same as a ride on the subway in Manhattan, only much safer.

Not totally convinced, but determined to get where she wanted to go, Mrs. Murphy forced a smile.

"Where do I sit?"

"Right there, ma'am."

Barry indicated one of the two back seats. The other was occupied by Mrs. Murphy's suitcase, securely strapped in.

"Mr. O'Leary and I will sit up front. Unless, of course, you want to be the pilot."

Barry's sense of humor again.

That left the front passenger seat for Tim, who climbed

in after Barry had settled into the pilot's spot. Both secured their harnesses, as did Mrs. Murphy, and Barry started the engine. After exchanging words with the tower, he moved the plane to the designated runway, and revved up the engine. The plane leaped forward and accelerated, picking up speed and straining to go airborne, until it lifted off the tarmac.

"We have lift-off!" Barry shouted over the drone of the engine.

Gaining altitude, the plane banked and turned north. They settled in for their flight to Millinocket.

"Look at the beautiful foliage!"

"It is gorgeous, Mrs. Murphy, isn't it? And look up ahead, that must be Katahdin."

"It is. It is! And it's getting closer. This view is breathtaking. Oh, Mr. O'Leary. I can't wait to see Hanny."

Barry looked up from the controls and took his earphones off.

"Hanny?"

"That's Mrs. Murphy's son, Barry. He's been on the Appalachian Trail with a group from Jay Peak. They should have come down from the mountain today. They're going over to Millinocket for a little celebration tonight, and then driving back to Jay tomorrow morning. Mrs. Murphy hasn't seen him in over three years."

"Three years to hike from Jay to Katahdin?"

"No, only the last seven or eight weeks. Before that he explored Central and South America, looking for clues from ancient civilizations–the Mayas, the Incas, the Aztecs."

"No kidding? Hey, Mrs. Murphy, how old is your boy?"

"My son is twenty-four years old, but he'll be twenty-five pretty soon."

"Well, wish him a happy birthday for me, ma'am."

The plane's radio crackled. Barry pulled on his headset.

"Eagle One here."

He paused, listening.

"Are you for real?"

He waited again.

"Roger."

The plane banked left.

"Sorry, folks. We've got little problem. We have to divert."

Another joke?

"Divert, Barry? What does that mean"

"It means we can't land at Millinocket. We've been diverted to Greenville."

"Greenville?"

"Yes. Greenville Municipal Airport. Sammy Cowan got himself a little juiced up and drove his pickup onto one of our runways a little while ago. Smacked into Truman's Piper Cub and spun it clear onto the other runway. Then it flipped over. Sammy's truck is all smashed up and leaking gas. The airport's closed. We've got to go to Greenville. I'll bet Truman's really pissed. That Piper's his baby."

Mrs. Murphy suddenly realized something was going on. The engine noise made it difficult to hear what was being said up front. Leaning forward, she tried to speak loudly enough to make herself heard.

"What's he saying, Mr. O'Leary? Why did we turn around?"

"We didn't turn around, Mrs. Murphy," Tim said over his shoulder. "We just changed direction somewhat. Barry says there's been an accident at the Millinocket airport, so we have to land at a different airport, in a town called Greenville."

"But Hanny's going to be in Millinocket. Can someone give us a ride over there? Is it close?"

"I don't know. Barry?"

"Sorry to be the bearer of bad news, folks, but the answer is really 'no.' If the roads were open, you could drive back south toward Guilford and then swing around the Wilderness and head up the road to Millinocket. That one isn't open, though. That's why you're on this plane. Wait a minute. It's getting a little bumpy. We can talk after I set this thing down."

The plane started bouncing and wobbling. Tim nervously gripped the arm rests on his seat, while in the back seat, Mrs. Murphy started sobbing, whether from fear or because her hopes of seeing her son seemed to be vanishing in the now cloudy sky.

But Barry was enjoying himself.

"We're rockin' and rollin' now, folks! Yeee-hah!"

The little plane hit an air pocket, and dropped toward the treetops, now only a few hundred feet below.

"Ride'em, cowboy! Yee-hah!"

Raindrops began pelting the windshield. Barry pulled back on the stick, and the plane lurched upward, leveled off, and then started a slow descent. The rain slowed just as the shiny wet surface of a runway appeared below them. A few seconds later, the wheels touched down, the plane bounced up, then dropped down again, and held the runway as Barry brought it to a halt, clearly enjoying himself.

"Welcome to Greenville, folks, and thank you for flying On Eagles Wings!"

Tim exhaled.

"We're okay, Mrs. Murphy. We're fine now. Don't cry. We're okay."

She sniffled and wiped her eyes.

Barry taxied the plane to a small hangar, whose doors were closed. A man in a coonskin cap and a hunting jacket signaled toward what appeared to be a parking spot next to the hanger. Maneuvering the plane toward the indicated location, Barry opened his window.

"Hey, Bus. Big mess over in Millie, heh?"

"Heard about it, Barry. Sammy's really done it this time. Truman's gonna kick his butt."

"Truman, hell, Bus. It's Truman's wife Sammy's got to worry about. Truman was going to fly her down to Portland for the weekend, to see her sister and do some shopping. She's probably chasing Sammy down Main Street with Truman's thirty-aught-six Springfield right now."

Tim tapped Barry on the shoulder.

"Uh, Barry? What do we do now?"

"Just a second, Tim. Bus, can you tie me down? I've got to get these people in out of the rain."

"Sure thing, Barry. Here, use my umbrella. You want Ricky to come over in his taxi?"

"Yeah, thanks." Barry clambered down from the plane, and reached in to grab the suitcase. "Looks like they're stuck here for the night. Road to Millinocket's closed. That's why I was flying them up there from Bangor International before we got diverted. Maybe they can spend the night at the Lodge."

"You mean Kineo View?"

"Yeah. No point trying the back road."

Mrs. Murphy was still sniffling, but this comment got her attention.

"What back road?"

"Oh, there's a road from here through Kokadjo that goes over the top and on to Millinocket. Seventy miles or so. Trouble is half of it's unpaved, and you never know when a few rockslides or washouts might stop you in your tracks. Better to wait until morning when I can fly you back to Bangor. You can try renting a car and driving up to Millinocket from there. Route Fifteen should have reopened by then."

"But my son will be gone."

"Ma'am, I don't know what to tell you. The back road isn't much more than a trail through The Wilderness. That's some mean ass country. Oh, sorry. Excuse the language."

"Don't worry about that, Barry. I've heard worse. You should meet my brother-in-law. And I've heard about The Wilderness. My son just hiked through there. That's why he's going to be in Millinocket this evening. Doesn't someone around here have one of those trucks that can take us over there on that back road?"

Tim decided to get involved before this went any further.

"Mrs. Murphy, that just sounds too risky. Why don't we

stay over at that lodge and get a good night's sleep? After all, we can call Jay and ask them to let the group know what we're doing, and see if they can get word to Hanny to sit tight in Millinocket until we arrive. Even if that's not workable, they could make sure he stays at Jay when the tour is over, so we can drive there from Bangor tomorrow. Maybe they can even give us a phone number for where he'll be staying in Millinocket tonight, so you can call him."

"Tim, I want to see him. Everything we've tried has backfired, but sooner or later our luck has to change. The last thing we should do is stop trying. We're so close. I want to keep going. Barry?"

Barry looked at Bus.

"Bus?"

BUS WAS SHORT FOR BUSTER, but of course Buster was not his name. That's what his father had called him, as in "Whadd-aya think you're doin,' Buster?" The father, a rugged me-chanic who worked primarily on trucks and tractors, was focused on discipline. This was all right with Bus, as long as it didn't involve too much schoolwork. That was the prov-ince of his soft-hearted mother, so Bus did his chores when his father was around, and fooled around the rest of the time. The end result was a rather abbreviated academic career, but a well-developed set of skills for operating, repairing, and maintaining heavy equipment. These were highly valued at the municipal airport, as well as by area contractors when economic cycles were in positive territory, which was the case at the moment. Northern Maine was exceedingly vulnerable to economic downturns, but for now, at least, the local econ-omy was humming along.

Bus agreed to take Tim and Mrs. Murphy "over the top" to Millinocket, but warned them that with only a few hours of daylight left, any major obstacles they encountered could not be cleared away until morning light, and that if that happened they would have to "hunker down around the camp-fire" until dawn. Tim remained reluctant, but Mrs. Murphy continued to assert herself, and Tim finally surrendered.

"You're the client, Mrs. Murphy, and the client is always right ... usually right? ... sometimes right? Oh well, good secretaries are hard to find. Let's go."

So, after a brief stop to use the restroom, Tim, Mrs. Murphy and Bus climbed into a big vehicle Bus brought around from the back of the hanger. It looked like a truck, given its hefty size, its huge tires and its bulky appearance, but it had faux wood paneling that made it resemble an overgrown version of a 1950s station wagon. Obviously proud of it, Bus told them it was the latest thing in off-road vehicles, a "Jeep Grand Wagoneer."

Tim and Mrs. Murphy climbed in. Tim had to admit the seats were comfortable, and Mrs. Murphy registered her approval as well.

"This is such a nice car, Bus. I feel safe in it. It's so big, but it looks like a station wagon. Is that what they call it?"

"They call it a sport utility vehicle, ma'am, but it's not like all those other SUVs that never touch down on anything but pavement. This one goes off road like there's nothing to it. And it's still comfy and cozy. Just got it this year. Glad you like it. Okay, everyone buckled in? Let's go!"

He hit the accelerator. The Jeep moved forward, proceeding across the tarmac and onto the street. They drove into the little town of Greenville and then turned north. The rain had stopped, allowing for a pleasant ride. A half an hour later they passed through another small town called Kokadjo. The sun began to set, the daylight fading as they came out of town and continued north.

"It might get a little bumpy now, folks. They haven't gotten around to paving all of the next twenty miles or so, but this baby can take it," Bus said, affectionately patting the dashboard.

He wasn't exaggerating, as the ride alternately went from

smooth to jarring during the next twenty minutes, the Jeep's headlights sweeping up and down. Tim could see the forest closing in on the road. Fewer and fewer structures and cleared spaces came into view, until there were none. Another ten minutes passed. Tim could hear Mrs. Murphy whispering prayers in the back seat.

"How long before Millinocket, Bus?" he said.

"Maybe another hour or so. The last thirty miles will be a breeze. We've just got to get through the rest of this section before I can open 'er up."

Just then, a horrible groaning sound reverberated somewhere outside. Bus slammed on the brakes, as a huge pine tree crashed down onto the road ahead.

"Damn."

— 27 —

THE TREE HAD A TRUNK whose diameter was about three feet, but whose limbs made the mass of branches and pine needles confronting the vehicle more than ten feet high. Leaving the headlights on, Bus got out of the car and stared up at the tangled, green mess. He shook his head.

"About the only good thing here is that it landed in front of us, not on us. Listen, folks, I've got a chain saw and some rope in the back of the car, but I can't risk cutting this thing until I have a little daylight to work with. All I'd need would be for one of these supporting branches to break off and the whole tree roll over on top of me. Even if that didn't happen, I'd run out of gas for the saw before I got anywhere near cutting through all the branches. I might be able to cut just through the base, but the rest of it could still roll back on us. We're going to have to stay here until morning, and it's going to get a little chilly before then. Got any warm clothes in that suitcase?"

Mrs. Murphy was beside herself, her steely resolve of a few hours ago totally shattered.

"Oh, this is all my fault. Oh, Mr. O'Leary, I'm so sorry.

Why was I so stupid? We should have just stayed put like you said. I'm so sorry."

Tim felt like agreeing with her, but he suppressed the temptation, and tried to soothe her instead.

"It's okay, Mrs. Murphy. It's okay. You just wanted to see your son. Nothing wrong with that. We'll be fine here."

Would they? He wasn't so sure, as he looked around in the darkness.

"You can lie down in the back seat. It's got plenty of room. And didn't you tell me at the airport that you had some warm clothes for Hanny in the suitcase? Maybe Bus and I could borrow some of them."

"I'll make us a campfire," Bus said. "It won't do much to keep the animals away, but at least we won't be in the pitch black all night. I've also got a blanket and a little tent in the back of the car, where I keep the other stuff. Why don't I set up the tent and throw the blanket in there? Then Tim and I can take turns tending the fire and napping in the tent. The lady can stretch out in the car. Sound good?"

"Sure, Bus. Mrs. Murphy, could we see if there's anything in the suitcase that Bus and I could use tonight?"

"Yes, of course, Mr. O'Leary, but would you take it out of the car? It's a little heavy."

Tim reached in and pulled out the suitcase. Mrs. Murphy unfastened the latches and opened it. Bus aimed his flashlight.

"Winnie the Pooh?" he said.

"Oh, that. Hanny loved his stuffed animal when he was little. See? It has his name—Hannibal—stitched on it. He took it to bed with him every night. I thought he might like to see it again. Isn't it cute?"

"Uh, Mrs. Murphy, how about the warm clothes you mentioned?" Tim said.

"Oh, yes. Silly me. Here, under the divider."

She removed the toy and pulled back a towel on which it had been resting, then lifted a panel, revealing a pile of neatly folded sweaters, sweatpants, sweatshirts, ski caps and assorted toiletries. She took one of the sweaters and pointed to the rest.

"Take whatever you need. They're all loose fitting, so hopefully they'll work for both of you."

Tim and Bus were soon bundled up in Hanny's clothes.

"That should work," Bus said. "Now let me get the fire started. Why don't you two sit inside the car while I'm doing that. There's an extra flashlight in the glove compartment that you can use if you need to step outside to ... you know."

After rolling a number of large stones into a circle, Bus walked off into the woods, and returned a short time later with an armful of twigs and branches. He piled them in a pyramidal stack inside the ring of stones, shoved some leaves in among the twigs, and lit a match. Within seconds, flames leaped out from the bottom of the stack. He made several more trips to fetch additional firewood, adding it to the blaze. When he was done, he waved to the others and called out, inviting them to join him.

"Campfires are always welcome out here, folks. Pull up a rock and sit down."

Tim and Mrs. Murphy got out of the car.

"I have a few bags of trail mix and a thermos in here," said Bus as he reached into the back seat area and retrieved them.

"There's a little stream about a hundred yards that way," he said, pointing into the blackness. "I'll dip the thermos into the stream to get us some nice cold water, and then come right back."

When Bus disappeared into the woods again, Tim and Mrs. Murphy made themselves as comfortable as could be expected on the stones piled around the fire. She spoke first.

"There are probably all kinds of wild animals around here," she said. "I'm scared to death."

"You really shouldn't worry," Tim said. "You'll be in the car, for one thing, and you'll have the flashlight if you need to step out for anything. Besides, either Bus or I will be awake and tending the fire all night long."

"I'm still scared."

"Here we go, folks."

Bus, who had returned, handed them each a bag of trail mix. He unscrewed the thermos cap, and filled it with water. Taking a drink, Tim found it surprisingly cool and fresh.

"Gosh, Bus. This is as good as the water from my tap at home. Maybe better."

"Yep. No water pollution up here."

Tim passed the cup to Mrs. Murphy, who took a hesitant sip and smiled.

"Thank you, Bus, and this trail mix is very ... pleasant."

Relaxing a bit, the three of them talked for a while, about Mrs. Murphy's son, Tim's law practice, and Bus's hunting exploits. An hour passed before they decided to call it a night. Mrs. Murphy retired to her sleeping quarters, or to the back seat of the Grand Wagoneer, to be precise. Tim crawled into the tent that Bus had set up. Bus, who'd volunteered to take the first watch, gathered more firewood from the forest.

* * *

Mrs. Murphy's scream shocked Tim out of a peaceful slumber.

"Help! Help! It's going to kill me! Help!"

A big black bear squatted on the hood of the Grand Wagoneer, scratching and pounding on the front windshield.

Tim jumped up and hit the top of the tiny tent with such force that it pulled the stakes free from the ground, and the tent fabric wrapped itself around him like a shroud on a mummy. He tried to extricate himself as he staggered toward the vehicle. Mrs. Murphy screamed even louder, as she saw this apparition moving in her direction.

More frightened than either of them, the bear jumped from the hood, abandoning its quest for the open bag of trail mix it had seen on the top of the dashboard, and scampered into the forest. Just then, Bus returned to the campfire with a new load of firewood. He burst out laughing.

"Told you the fire wouldn't keep the critters away. I think you gave that one the scare of her life. She's gonna need some pills to get to sleep next month."

Tim finally extricated himself from the tent wrapped around him.

"Sleep?"

"You know, hibernate. October's when they start up here. Well, maybe she'll find some campers who'll share their meds with her."

Mrs. Murphy was awake the rest of the night.

28

THE SKIES STARTED TO LIGHTEN around six in the morning. Bus was still asleep in the tent, but Tim and Mrs. Murphy were wide awake. She sat in the back seat of the car, and Tim stood outside, watching the campfire, which was now burning itself out. He stepped over to the car, opened the front door, and looked in.

"That tree is big, isn't it, Mrs. Murphy? I guess Bus will know how to handle it."

"Well, I pray he does," she said.

"I'm going to give him a few more minutes, and then I'll wake him up. I'm sure we'll be on our way pretty soon."

"Oh, please God. I just couldn't sleep. I thought we were going to die out here."

"I know, but the worst is over now."

Tim hoped he sounded convincing, but he had experienced some of the same feelings himself during the long night. He walked over to the tent.

"Bus? It's morning. Time to get up."

A minute or so passed, and Tim decided he'd better try again, but there was a stirring inside the tent, and Bus's head emerged between the tent flaps.

"Morning already?"

"Sun's almost up, Bus. I thought we should start figuring how to get out of here."

"Guess so. What's for breakfast?"

Bus crawled out of the tent.

"Let me take a look at this monster, Tim."

He walked over to the tree's massive root ball, which held the base of the trunk a few feet off the ground. Part of the base was cracked, probably from the leveraging effect of the upper mass of the tree as it crashed down onto the road. There were some signs of rot inside the trunk.

"Beautiful old white pine, Tim. Looks like a good gust of wind left over from yesterday's storm must have administered the coup de grâce."

"You speak French, Bus?"

"Nah, just a couple of the words I've picked up from the Canadian trappers when they sneak down from Kee-beck. Anyway, this is a mess, in any language."

He stopped for a few minutes, apparently considering the options. Then he continued.

"I might be able to saw through the base, but that's it," he said. "Not enough fuel for anything more. If I do that, we can tie one end of a rope around the top of the tree and attach the other end to my truck. I have a towing package on the back."

Tim noticed Bus was now referring to his vehicle as a "truck," and doing so with some fondness. Apparently, it was no longer a glorified taxicab.

"Then I'll drag the tree by its top section, and it should pivot around that big heavy base until enough of the road is clear for us to drive past. Should work. There's a 5.9 liter V8 under that truck's hood. It can tow its own weight, two and a half tons, and we're not haulin' it anywhere, just pullin' it outta' the way. Let's get going."

Bus opened the back of the Grand Wagoneer and extracted a heavy rope and a long case. He carried both to the side of the road, where he dropped the rope before unfastening the latches on the case and opening it. Inside was a chainsaw with a blade that Tim thought might be as much as three feet long. Bus hauled it out and brandished it like a weapon to be used for the battle ahead.

"Stihl, Tim. The best there is, in my opinion. It should handle that tree trunk easy. Before I go to work, though, why don't you back up the truck and turn it around. I don't want the tree to roll on top of it when I cut through the base. Might get a scratch or two. Key's in the glove compartment."

Tim did as instructed, moving the vehicle to face down the road in the direction from which they had come the evening before. He was too nervous to do it with the classic three-point turn, but managed to complete the process after several cautious starts and stops. In the meantime, Bus was checking the fuel and oil in his chain saw, and inspecting the downed tree to see if it looked stable enough not to roll when it broke loose from its massive stump. Satisfied, he started up the saw and went to work. Carefully and methodically, he cut in stages and at different angles to avoid having the trunk close up on the chainsaw's blade, imprisoning it and ending their hopes of driving on to Millinocket. He ultimately succeeded in severing the trunk from the base. The tree sighed and settled down on its branches.

"Okay, Tim, time to wrap this baby up. I'm goin' around to the other side. When I get there, I'm gonna tie this rope to some of the bottom branches about halfway up the tree. Then I'm gonna throw it over the top. If it comes over clear, holler, and I'll come back. If it doesn't, let me know and I'll pull it loose and try again. Got it?"

"Yes, Bus."

"Okay. Off I go."

In short order, Bus had accomplished what he set out to do. He threw the rope over the top, and returned to Tim's side of the tree. He grabbed the end of the rope that he had thrown over to Tim, walked it back to the Jeep, and hooked it onto the towing bar beneath the rear bumper. That done, he took another section of rope out of the Jeep and, without attaching it to the vehicle, carried it with him as he returned to the fallen tree. Tying this one securely to several branches in the upper section of the side facing them, he wound it through a few more branches closer to the top. He then dropped the loose end on the ground fifteen or twenty feet from the tree as he strolled back toward the vehicle.

What he had in mind became clear a few minutes later, as he got into the Jeep, started it up, and moved it slowly down the road away from the fallen tree. The first rope, which he had attached to the branches in the tree's middle section on the opposite side, went taut, and the tree began slowly to roll in the same direction as the vehicle was heading. Eventually, the tree had rolled sufficiently so that the knotted attachment point of the first rope came into sight at the top, and then gradually descended, until that rope was parallel to the ground, tautly stretched from its attachment point in the middle section of the tree to the rear of the vehicle. Bus turned off the engine, got out of the car, walked around to the back, and unhooked the first rope.

Tim was intrigued, but mystified. Mrs. Murphy, who had been quietly watching from a safe distance, came over.

"What is he doing, Mr. O'Leary?"

"I really don't know, Mrs. Murphy, but he obviously has a plan."

Bus returned to the tree. The end of the second rope was now wrapped three-quarters of the way around the tree, as a result of tree having rolled over it as the Jeep moved down the road. He attached a clamp to the rope at the point where he had attached it to the branches, and then he threaded the loose end of the rope through the clamp, so that the rope now totally encircled the top section of the tree. He unhooked several other clamps which were attached to his belt, and, reaching into the heart of the top of the tree, he methodically attached as many of the branches as he could to the rope, tightening each connection. Then he grabbed the loose end of the rope and played it out behind him as he walked back toward them.

The whole process, starting with the chainsaw phase, had taken nearly three hours.

"That should do it, folks. Why don't you come back to the truck with me so you can watch the show?"

Tim and Mrs. Murphy followed Bus to the Wagoneer. They stood to the side, as Bus attached the rope to the towing bar at the rear of the vehicle. He jumped in, started it up, and drove it slowly down the road, away from the tree. The rope pulled tight, strained, and then began to tug the treetop, which followed behind like an obedient dog. The entire tree began to pivot, as the top moved along, while the base stayed where it was. Slowly but surely, the massive pine rotated clockwise, and eventually came to rest on the shoulder of the road directly behind the Jeep. There was now a modest, but sufficiently wide, space on the opposite side to allow the vehicle to pass, with only a manageable portion of that shoulder to traverse, and that would be no problem for a Grand Wagoneer.

Tim was delighted. Mrs. Murphy, realizing they had been freed from their forest prison, started to sigh with relief. Suddenly, she stopped, gasped, and shrieked. Someone was standing in the road ahead.

"Hi, Mom!"

A smiling Hanny stood in the middle of the road, at the forefront of a group of young men and women. Visible behind them was a rugged looking bus, from which the group had presumably emerged. Mrs. Murphy ran toward her son, as he approached her, smiling.

They wrapped their arms around one another.

"Honey, Honey! It's my boy! Honey, I came to find you. Oh, Honey. Oh, my lord, I haven't called you that since you were a little boy. I've been so worried. Are you all right?

How did you get here?"

The group behind him had no idea what was going on, but the scene was irresistible, and they spontaneously burst into applause. Tim and Bus joined in, as did the bus driver, who had stepped down onto the road as the scene unfolded. Everyone was smiling, and a few of the girls wiped tears from their eyes.

29

"HEY, AL!" The bus driver was calling out to Bus.

Bus walked over to where the driver was standing, and they began to talk, while the hikers closed in around Mrs. Murphy and Hanny, chatting excitedly, obviously intrigued by this unexpected encounter.

A few minutes later, Bus came back and took Tim aside.

"Rick has an idea."

"The bus driver?"

"Yeah."

"He called you Al."

"He's a wise guy. Thinks that's funny."

"Why did he do it?"

"It's my name."

"I thought your name was Bus."

"That's what I go by, but that's not the name on my birth certificate."

"What would that be?"

"Algernon."

"Are you kidding?"

"Now, don't you start. It was my mother's idea. Not too

many people know about it, and the ones who do, they know I don't like it. I bet your boy Hannibal has the same problem with his moniker. Smart alecks like Rick think they're being funny when they remind me of mine. Enough, let's change the subject. Anyway, Rick the comedian has an idea. I think you should go for it."

"Tell me."

"Well, first of all, you should hear how the bus happened to be coming down this road."

"I was wondering about that."

"The causeway was still blocked this morning, so Rick decided to drive the hiking party over the top and take the long route from Kokadjo to Jay Peak. His bus is equipped for off road, and he figured it was better than waiting until the locals finally got around to clearing the causeway. He made it this far a little while ago, and then he saw the big white pine blocking the way. He stepped out to take a look, and, lo and behold, the tree started to move. His passengers got out too, and before you knew it, there we were! Or at least there your Mrs. Murphy was. You know the rest."

Wow. Who would have guessed?"

"Don't underestimate the power of a mother, my man. I mean, Algernon? Come on."

"So, what's his idea?"

"He says there's no point in me taking you the rest of the way to Millinocket, since what you're looking for is right here. He has room in his bus for you and the boy's mother, and he can take you to Jay Peak with the rest of the hikers. You'll have to pay, of course, and you and I will have to settle up also, now that I think of it. I'll just turn around and drive back to Greenville, and we'll all wind up where we want to be. Sound good?"

"Mrs. Murphy will be delighted."

"Great. Oh, and here's the clincher."

"What's that?"

"The bus has a toilet."

"Done. I'll go tell Mrs. Murphy."

Tim and Mrs. Murphy bade farewell to Bus. They thanked him, paid him, and boarded Rick's bus.

Once everyone was settled in, the bus started up and squeezed past the felled pine tree. They then continued along the bumpy road for twenty miles or so, until they reached the little town named Kakadjo that they had driven through the day before. There they made a rest stop and took a bathroom break (the toilet on the bus had its limitations), and then continued on their way. Before leaving the town, Tim used a pay phone outside the general store to call Marge and let her know what had happened. He said he'd tell her the whole story when he saw her, but for now he reassured her that everyone was fine. He thought they'd better stay overnight in Jay, so they could get some rest. He'd rent a car there, and drive them home the next day.

The hikers were coming off a late night celebrating their long trek, and most fell asleep soon after the bus drove out of Kokadjo. Mrs. Murphy finally succumbed to sleepiness herself, and nodded off as well, as did Tim. Hanny seemed tireless, however. Leaving the seat next to his mother, he moved up to the front of the bus and engaged Rick in conversation while the others slept.

At one point, Mrs. Murphy shifted her position to get more comfortable, and opened her eyes for a moment. When she saw the empty seat next to her, she gasped.

"Oh, no. Oh, no. It was all a dream. Oh no."

Her outburst woke Tim, who looked over from across the aisle.

"Mrs. Murphy, what's the matter? Did you have a bad dream?"

"It's Hanny. I thought we had found him, but we didn't. He's not here at all. It was all a dream. Oh, no."

"Mrs. Murphy, we did find him. See? He's up there talking to the bus driver."

She craned her neck to look.

"Oh, thank goodness. I thought … I don't know what I thought. I'm awful. I'm sorry."

"It's okay. Everything's fine, now. Just go back to sleep. We have a long trip ahead of us."

"Yes, yes. I'll do that." She closed her eyes.

Tim knew he wouldn't be able to sleep now, so he got up and walked forward.

"Hey, Rick. How are we doing?"

"Not bad. Another five hours or so. It would've been quicker to go through Canada, but none of these kids have passports with them. I'm guessing you guys don't, either."

"You're right about that. I never guessed when we left New York yesterday that we'd wind up in Canada, or in a place called Kokadjo, for that matter. Pretty town, though, and pretty country. Maybe my wife and I should bring the kids up there next year."

"Yeah, Maine is one of the last of the unspoiled places, for sure. And we're heading for another—Vermont."

Hanny was smiling.

"It may be the place I've been looking for, Mr. O'Leary. I've been happy ever since I got there. I think I may stay."

"Call me Tim, Hanny. I can't seem to get your mother to do that, but I'd like it if you would. After all, you might be my client soon."

"Your client?"

"Yes. Let's take a couple of those empty seats in the back of the bus, and I can tell you what's been going on."

30

"HANNY, YOUR FATHER DIED."

"What? When? Why didn't my mother tell me?"

"I think she was so overjoyed about finding you this morning, she didn't even think to tell you. I'm sure she would have. It's been about two years now since he died. It happened after you went away, and about a year after you were last in contact with your mother. There was a car accident. I'm sorry to be the one to have to give you the bad news."

Hanny dropped his gaze to his hands, which were clenched on his lap.

"He and I didn't always get along, Mr. O'Leary, Tim I mean. My dad thought I should be more organized, get my degree, look for a job. He was right, of course, but I felt there was something more out there for me, something worth looking for, and I wanted to find it. I guess I was being selfish, and maybe a little naive, but I knew I had to try. You know, it's funny, but I think I may have finally found what I was looking for, and I planned to tell him when I saw him. I guess I won't be able to now."

Hanny's voice caught, and he fell silent for a moment.

"Did he suffer?"

"I'm afraid so, Hanny. It was several months before the injuries he sustained in the accident finally took his life. A painful several months, from what I've been told."

"I feel so guilty."

"Don't, Hanny. It wasn't your fault, and I don't think your father would have wanted you to blame yourself for an accident you had nothing to do with. He clearly cared about you, so much, in fact, that he left you his entire estate under his Will."

"He did?"

"Yes, and that's why I wanted to talk to you."

Tim told Hanny about the lawsuit, and about how the settlement funds were allocated in a way that made them payable entirely to his father's estate, rather than to Hanny directly. He told him that his uncle Chris was named executor of the estate, and how his uncle's animosity toward Hanny and his mother was causing complications in getting the estate wound up.

"Yes, I know he doesn't like mom, but I don't know why. Uncle Chris had some financial problems once, and I think my mother talked my dad out of lending him money. She thought their savings should be used for my education when the time came for me to go to college. Maybe that, and the fact that I screwed up when that time did come, turned my uncle against both of us. I have a feeling there was more to it, though, but I just don't know."

"Whatever the reason, it's clearly the way he feels," Tim said. "I called him recently and told him you were back in the States. I asked him to get things ready so that your father's estate administration could be wrapped up, and the money could be turned over to you. This conversation, if you want to call it that, was a very short one. I had barely gotten the words out of my mouth when he made some disparaging remarks about your mother, and about you, and then he hung up on me. A little bit later on, I found out something else, and I called him again."

"What was that?"

"Your mother showed me a copy of your father's Will, and I saw that you weren't to receive the money right away. If you weren't twenty-five yet, it was to be held in trust for you until you reached that age. The Will appointed your mother to be trustee of the trust. Given that, I had her authorize me to take steps to compel your uncle to turn over the estate assets to the trust. That's why I called him the second time."

"How did he react to that?"

"Pretty much the same way, and he said the trust would end soon, anyway, and that when it did, the funds couldn't go to you. He said that you weren't competent to handle large sums of money, and that he was going to have himself appointed as your guardian so he could manage them for you."

"Can he do that?"

"Not if we can help it. In the meantime, I've started a lawsuit that asks the court to force him to tell your mother what he's been doing with your father's estate, and to turn everything over to your mother as your trustee, without further delay."

"Will that work?"

"Normally, I would say yes, but there's one problem."

"What's that?"

"The trust is going to end very soon. You're almost twenty-five, and your uncle can probably stall this thing long enough to have the court dismiss the suit on the grounds that the trust terminated when you reached that age, and that the trust is no longer the beneficiary."

"So, things don't look good then?"

"That depends on you."

"On me? What can I do?"

"You can get involved. If you join with your mother in the litigation, your uncle's argument becomes moot. It's either the trustee or you who is entitled to the estate, and as executor he'll be ordered to account for what he's received, what he's done with it, and what's there now. If he's done a good job, he can take his commissions and turn over what's left to you, or, if you're not twenty-five yet, to your mother as your trustee."

"This is an awful lot for me to absorb, Tim. How much time do I have?"

"The case is on the court's calendar next Friday."

Hanny drew a long breath and exhaled.

"Is there much money involved? My father never had a lot. I guess the car accident case might have added some, but there must have been lots of medical expenses. What do you think could be there now for me?

"There should be over two million dollars."

"Two million?"

"Yes. The lawsuit settled for six million, and all the medical expenses. The lawyer took a third of the six, the IRS grabbed its share, and the rest went into the estate."

"Oh, my God. What do I have to do?"

"Why don't you talk to your mother about your getting involved. If she's comfortable with it, and if you are too, I will represent both of you in the proceeding we just started, and in anything that follows. Essentially, you will step into the trustee's shoes as soon as you turn twenty-five, and given that, I don't think there would be any conflict in me representing both of you. That is, of course, if she hasn't prejudiced your interests by not acting sooner to protect them."

"Don't worry about that, Tim. She would never act against my best interests."

"I'm sure she wouldn't do so intentionally, Hanny, but we'll have to see what your uncle's been up to these last couple of years, before we can know for sure. Right now, though, I think it would be best if you come back home so we can do the paperwork, and then I'd like to have both of you with me in court next week."

"Can we stop at Jay first?"

"Sure. I think we're all going to be too tired to leave for home tonight. We'll get a couple of rooms and stay over, then head out tomorrow morning. I'll rent a car."

"All right. I guess this is something I have to do, but I'll need to call Margaret first."

"Am I thinking of the same Margaret? The one who works at the border?"

"Yes. She was one of the customs officers at the border crossing when I came down from Canada. She's really nice. She gave me a ride to Jay and helped me line up some work there. That's how I wound up on the Appalachian Trail hike. We went out to eat that night, and I promised her I'd call when I got back."

31

MRS. MURPHY ARRIVED in the office early on Friday, determined to work "right through the weekend" if necessary to bring everything up to date after her three-day absence. She couldn't stop smiling as she typed away at the keyboard.

"You look happy this morning, Mrs. M."

Tim's partner Mike Green had emerged from his office with an empty coffee mug in his hand.

"Oh, I certainly am, Mr. Green. I certainly am. Did you hear the news?"

"I sure did. Tim called me last night. He said your boy is coming in to see us this morning."

"Yes, he is. He was just going to stop at the bank first to open an account, and deposit his paycheck for the hiking expedition."

"Tim also told me you're quite the camper yourself. Faced down a big bear in the wilderness. Ran her off with her tail between her legs."

"Stop that now, Mr. Green. I was terrified. I won't be going on any more camping adventures. You can be sure of that."

"No, seriously? I was thinking you and Hanny could

show me and my wife the ropes. We were planning on doing some camping ourselves next year. You'd be the perfect
person to lead us into the unknown. Why don't you give it
some thought? It's in your blood now. You might change
your mind."

He walked away chuckling, and went to get more coffee.

"Good morning, Mrs. Murphy."

Tim had arrived, with Hanny only a few steps behind.

"Good morning to you, Mr. O'Leary. Isn't it a beautiful
morning? And Hanny! Oh, it's just so wonderful seeing you
here. Let me get coffee for both of you. I'll bring it into your
office, Mr. O'Leary."

"None for me, Mom. Unless you've got some of that dark
Columbian. I picked up a lot of bad habits down in South
America. Anyway, I won't be staying long. Tim just wanted
me to come in to sign some papers. Then I'm going to the
library to look at job listings in the newspapers."

Tim smiled. "Good for you, Hanny. Why don't you come
into my office for a minute?"

Hanny followed Tim into his office and sat across from
him, as Tim looked through some documents that had accu-
mulated during his absence. He pushed aside a stack of mail
and looked over papers prepared by the part-time secretary,
Mrs. Turner, and the temp Mrs. Murphy had brought in to
cover for her while they went to Maine. Finding the docu-
ment he was searching for, he passed it over to Hanny.

"This is an authorization for me to appear on your behalf
in the lawsuit we've instituted against your uncle. I called
Mrs. Turner before we left Jay yesterday morning and asked
her to type it up. I wanted to get your signature on it before
you headed out this morning."

"What does that mean, 'appear?'"

"It means I will act as your attorney. Basically, we're suing your uncle, to make him tell us what's been going on in
your father's estate. We want him to finish up whatever he's
doing, and then pay everything out to your mother as your

trustee, or to you of course, if you've turned twenty-five by the time that happens."

"Do you think he'll do it?"

"He'll have to."

"Then why hasn't he done it already?"

"Good question. At the very least, he likes controlling the money, and getting paid while he does."

"And at worst?"

"That's the scary part."

"You mean he might have stolen it?"

"Let's hope not. One way or the other, though, he's made it very clear that he's not going to do anything voluntarily. He's even threatened to ask the court to appoint him as your guardian, so he can manage your money indefinitely. He says you're not competent to do it yourself."

"Maybe he's right. I don't know how to handle money, especially that much money."

"No one says you do, at least not yet, but you have a right to know what he's been up to with your father's estate, and to have him turn the estate assets over to you, so you can make your own decisions on how the money should be handled from now on."

"Would you be able to help with that?"

"You mean the investment decisions?"

"Yes."

"No, but I'll help you find someone. What I'm doing is trying to force your uncle to account for what he's done, hand over what's there, and make good for any losses you've suffered if he's done anything wrong."

Hanny leaned over and looked at the paper.

"And you'll do that if I sign this?"

"I will."

"May I have a pen?"

"Right here, Hanny."

Hanny signed the authorization and sat back.

"Is that it?"

"That's it, Hanny. We'll have your signature notarized on this before you go."

"What's next?" Hanny said.

"After I dropped you and your mom at home last evening, I stopped by here and dictated the motion papers on our office recording equipment. We're asking the court to allow you to participate in the lawsuit. Your mother is typing them up right now. As soon as the papers are typed, I'll sign them, go over to the courthouse, and file them. That way, we'll be all set when the case is on the calendar next Friday."

32

A WEEK LATER, Tim left his home in Connecticut and drove to the Bronx, where he would appear before the surrogate on the return date of the proceeding they had instituted against Chris Murphy.

The building housing the Bronx County Surrogate's Court was located on the Grand Concourse, a few blocks from Yankee Stadium. Given its proximity to "The House that Ruth Built," Mike Green, a rabid Yankees fan, considered offering to make the initial court appearance in the Murphy matter. When he checked the schedule, however, he realized the Yanks were to play a night game that Friday. There being no point in killing time in the South Bronx all afternoon, he decided to pass on the opportunity, and told Tim that he had a conflict, or he would have been delighted to do it. Tim didn't recall having suggested to Mike that he cover the matter for him, but he politely thanked him and continued to prepare for the appearance.

The court had recently lost its judge, Bertram Gelfand, in a scandal that had resulted in his removal from the bench. The state's highest court found that he had "misused his position as Surrogate of Bronx County by making administrative and personnel decisions, taking official actions and making implicit and explicit threats to court officials and others in order to prolong a sexual relationship with a law assistant and later to exact personal vengeance when she refused to continue their affair."

Gelfand, who had otherwise been considered an excellent judge by those who practiced before him, would therefore not be there on Friday to preside over the Murphy case. In his place would be the head of the court's law department, Lee Holtzman, who would shortly become the new Surrogate, having won a contested primary to be the Democratic party's candidate to succeed Gelfand in the upcoming election. Election day was considered to be a mere formality in this regard, since no one could recall the last time a Republican had won anything in the Bronx. Even the wealthy "Bronx Bombers," the New York Yankees, some of whom were surely Republicans, hadn't won a World Series in ten years.

Tim had asked Mrs. Murphy to bring Hanny with her to the courthouse, and to arrive half an hour before the 9:30 a.m. call of the calendar. She did him one better, and had already been sitting in the courthouse cafeteria for nearly forty-five minutes when Tim walked in at nine.

"Mrs. Murphy, Hanny, good morning. How are you both?"

"Nervous, Mr. O'Leary, very nervous. What do you think my brother-in-law will say to the judge about me? Will I have to say anything? Do you think the judge will be annoyed at us for taking up his time? Is—"

"Mrs. Murphy, just stay calm. You won't have to say anything. I just want you there in case any decisions have to be made this morning, and I need your consent or your son's before making them."

"Decisions? What kind of decisions? I'm not good at making decisions. Oh, I'm so nervous."

"Relax, Mom."

Hanny stood up and extended his hand to Tim.

"Morning, Tim. Mom's very nervous, as you can see. I told her not to worry, that you'll take good care of us. Besides, this is just about money, and if I've learned anything these last five years, it's that money isn't the answer."

"You're right about that, Hanny, but I'd rather see your father's money in your hands, the way he wanted, and not in your uncle's. Let's sit down and talk about what we should expect to happen today."

For the next ten minutes, Tim explained the procedure that would be followed in the courtroom that morning.

The three of them would sit in the spectator section until the judge arrived, at which point the court attendant would shout the familiar "All rise. The Surrogate's Court of Bronx County is now in session," followed by whatever he liked to add, such as "all those who have business before the court may come forward when your matter is called," or something along those lines.

The judge, or whoever was going to preside over the calendar call, seeing as there was no surrogate at the moment, would then tell them to be seated, and the call of the calendar would begin. Their case would be relatively far down the calendar, so they would probably have at least a fifteen or twenty-minute wait before it was called. When the time came, Tim would stand up and identify himself.

Assuming he was there, Hanny's uncle Chris would do the same, at which point the two attorneys would be instructed to come forward and give their full names, and the names of their clients, to the court's stenographer. They'd be asked to explain their respective positions, after which the court would decide what should happen next.

Tim assumed Chris would not consent to anything. If that proved to be the case, the court would either direct Chris to prepare an accounting and give him a specific date when the account would be due, or, perhaps, send the attorneys to see someone in the court's law department to explore the possibilities of resolving the matter without litigation.

"Okay, that's it. It's as simple as that," Tim said. "Do you have any questions before we go up to the courtroom?"

"I don't. Mom?"

"No, I don't, Hanny. I just wish it was over."

"It will be before you know it, Mrs. Murphy. Let's go."

The three of them stood up, and Tim showed them the way to the courtroom. Once there, they took seats and waited. Not long afterwards, a door opened in the front of the courtroom, and members of the court's staff began to file in. Then, as predicted, one of them announced that everyone should rise. As they did, a middle-aged gentleman entered the courtroom, climbed the few steps to the judge's chair, and sat down.

"Good morning, everyone. Please be seated. My name is Lee Holtzman. I'm the court's chief law assistant, and as such I'm responsible for the court's law department. I will be presiding over the calendar today, there being no judge of this court at the present time. A new surrogate will be elected in November, and then sworn in after the first of the year. In the meantime, if any orders or decrees need to be issued, a judge from one of our other courts has been assigned the responsibility of taking care of that. Will the clerk kindly call the calendar?"

The calendar call proceeded as predicted, and after nearly a half hour, the clerk called out their case.

"Estate of Francis Murphy."

Tim stood.

"For the petitioner, Madeline Murphy," he said, "and for the movant, Hannibal Murphy."

Other than a few titters from the spectators, presumably at the mention of Hannibal's name, no one else spoke. Mr. Holtzman waited several seconds, and then, looking around, asked, "Is the respondent Christopher Murphy present?"

No one responded.

"Please come forward, sir," Holtzman said, signaling to

Tim, "and put your appearance on the record."

Tim complied.

"Mr. O'Leary, have you heard from the respondent?" Holtzman asked, referring to Chris Murphy.

"No, your honor, I have not. The last time we spoke was when I called to advise him that we were instituting this proceeding."

"Did he give you any indication as to whether he would be submitting his accounting."

"No, your honor, he did not. To the contrary, he made it quite clear he had no intention of accounting to the trustee."

"All right, let's hold this until second call. Hopefully, he just got stuck in traffic. We all know how that can happen. In the meantime, I'll have someone in the law department call his office, just to make sure he didn't get confused about the date."

Holtzman nodded to one of the members of the court's law department standing nearby.

"Ms. Logan, would you make that call? Here, take the file with you."

The call of the calendar resumed.

Tim returned to his seat, and asked Mrs. Murphy and her son to step out to the hallway with him.

Once outside, he tried to explain what had happened.

"As I think you noticed, Chris didn't show up for the calendar call. I don't think we're going to see him on second call, either."

"Second call? What does that mean?" Hanny asked.

"It just means they'll call the matters that weren't resolved when the calendar was called the first time. These would include those where someone was delayed, and missed the first call."

"When does second call happen?"

"Probably in the next twenty or thirty minutes, but as I said, something tells me we're not going to see your uncle Chris then, either. Let's just wait and see."

They didn't have to wait until second call to find out.

33

"THEY PHONED HIS OFFICE and got his secretary. She said Chris hadn't been there in over a week. She knew about the court date and tried several times to reach him at home, but no one answered."

Tim and Marge were sitting in their living room, while Timmy did his homework upstairs, and Katie played with her new Kermit the Frog and Miss Piggy dolls in the next room. Tim was worried. Marge was intrigued.

"What happens now? What about the money?" Marge said.

"Mr. Holtzman, who by the way will soon be Judge Holtzman since he has the Democratic party's nomination, said they would sign an order compelling Chris to account. If he doesn't do so within thirty days after the order is served on him, he'll be removed as executor."

"How will you serve it on him if no one knows where he is?"

"That's the problem."

"Why don't I see what I can do. I've got a few contacts in the area who might be able to help, but to tell you the truth,

I'd be more worried about the money than Chris's where-abouts if I were you. Who cares if Chris took off? Good rid-dance. The money is another story. If he made off with it, you've got a much bigger problem."

"I know, Marge. This is bad."

"Did Chris post bond as executor?"

"No."

"Do we have any idea where the estate account is main-tained?"

"No again."

"How do we find out?"

"Mike suggested we submit an order for the court to sign, directing Chris's law firm to make the estate account records available for our inspection."

"Chris's firm? I thought he was a solo practitioner."

"That's right, but we think he formed a professional cor-poration. It's commonly done, to protect the lawyer's per-sonal assets against judgments not involving the law practice itself. We noticed that his listing in the yellow pages reads 'Christopher P. Murphy, P.C.'"

"Okay, but he's still the only person in his firm. Don't you have to serve the order on a corporate officer? In other words, on him?"

"We're hoping he made his secretary an officer, so she could sign things and save him the trouble."

"And if he didn't?"

"One problem at a time, Marge."

"I know. There has to be some way to find him, though. Give me a little time. I'll think of something. In the mean-time, we'd better get ready."

"Get ready for what?"

"Parent teacher night at Katie's school."

"Parent teacher night? Katie's only in kindergarten."

"I guess they want to educate us about how they're going to educate her. We'd better go, or they might be annoyed, and take it out on Katie."

"You mean tell her that if her parents really loved her they would have made sure she had a Baby Fozzie doll, too, like all the other kids?"

"Very funny, Tim. Let's go."

* * *

Halloween decorations were already starting to show up at Darien's Hindley School, even though the holiday was about a month away. The school was on the Post Road, only a few blocks from the church they attended on Sundays. Tim concluded that the Halloween motif must have been more appealing to the school's age ten and under student body than a Columbus Day theme, which could be found nowhere in sight.

After signing in at the front desk, they walked down the hallway to their daughter's classroom, and did their best to squeeze into the children's tiny chairs. Marge eventually succeeded, but Tim gave up and decided to stand instead. Most of the other parents did the same, as they waited for the teacher to arrive, which she did a few minutes later.

"Good evening, everyone. My name is Maddy Trainor, and I'm your children's kindergarten teacher. Welcome to what may be your first parent-teacher night. I apologize for the seating arrangements."

Chuckles from the parents.

"Please make yourselves as comfortable as possible, while I give you a brief overview of what we'll be trying to accomplish during the year. Then I'll be speaking briefly to a few of you that I wanted to meet with privately this evening, for various reasons."

The smiles on many of the parents' faces turned to looks of concern. Perhaps some children were having behavioral issues that Miss Trainor wanted to discuss with mom and dad?

"The others are free to tour the school with one of our fifth graders, who have volunteered to act as guides for any new parents who would like an introduction to our wonderful facility. There are also some special exhibits you might enjoy seeing. They're in the library, where several of our class mothers have joined us this evening. They would love to fill you in on the many volunteer opportunities for mothers and fathers here at Hindley. So, let me tell you about what to expect this year."

Miss Trainor spoke for fifteen minutes about the curriculum, which was surprisingly extensive for what at one time was little more than a year of playing with blocks and drawing pictures with crayons. Then, with a kindly nod, she thanked them for coming. She said she would always be available to meet with any parents who might have questions about their child's progress. Everyone was free, she added, to look around the classroom or the school while she met with a few of them in her office down the hall.

"Are Katie O'Leary's parents here?"

Tim and Marge, not a little surprised, raised their hands.

"Oh, good. Would the two of you come with me? I will also be speaking with the Cavanaughs, if they could stay behind for a few minutes. I'll stop back to get you as soon as I'm finished speaking with the O'Learys."

"What's this about, Marge?" Tim whispered, as they followed the teacher down the hall to her office.

"I have no idea, Tim. I hope Katie didn't get herself in trouble. She can be pretty rambunctious at times."

"Yikes. This could be the start of a long year," Tim said.

Miss Trainor stopped at the door to her office, unlocked it, and invited them in. The room was quite small, with barely enough space for a small desk, a bookshelf, and three chairs. She took the one behind the desk, and gestured toward the other two.

"Please. Sit down. I hope you have a few minutes."

"Of course, Miss Trainor. This is something of a surprise. My husband and I hope Katie isn't causing problems in the class. If she is, we will speak to her as soon as we get home."

The teacher smiled.

"There's no need to be upset. Now just sit and we can talk."

They sat down, pleased at least that these were grown up size chairs.

"So, what has she done, Miss Trainor? My wife and I both work. Sometimes it makes us feel guilty that we're not home enough for the kids. Maybe we could try to take turns working from home. Do you think that could help? We'll do whatever it takes. We had no idea Katie was misbehaving."

"Mr. And Mrs. O'Leary, please. It's nothing like that. Katie just has to learn how to act. That's what I wanted to speak to you about."

"That's what we were afraid of, although to be honest with you, she is a lively little devil, but we never thought she'd be a problem in school, did we, Marge?"

"No, Tim, we didn't, but I guess we must have missed something. Miss Trainor, what do you suggest we do?"

The teacher started to laugh.

"What I'm trying to tell you is that we want Katie to play Zuzu in the high school drama club's Christmas play. She's perfect for the part of the Baileys' littlest child in *It's a Wonderful Life*."

Tim looked at Marge.

"She's so cute, and we think she's bright enough to learn the part. Of course, we need your consent."

"And that's why she has to learn how to act?" Marge said.

"That's why she has to learn how to act."

34

"SHE SAYS SHE'S A SECRETARY, not an officer," Mike said.

"A secretary is an officer. You know, president, vice president, secretary, treasurer."

"Not this one. This is the kind that knows how to type."

"So, where do we go from here?"

"I don't know, Tim. Without someone to serve, the order directing Murphy to make the estate records available to us isn't much more than a piece of paper. And even if we can get the court to suspend his letters, whoever steps in to take over the estate will be operating in a vacuum. We have no idea what assets are in the estate or where they're held. Something interesting happened yesterday, though."

Just then, Mrs. Murphy walked in with the draft of the order Mike had asked her to type. She handed it to him.

"Do you need anything else, either of you? I promised Hanny I'd have lunch with him today. He's going up to Vermont tomorrow to see that young lady he met while he was there. He said he might stay for a little while to find out if there are any job opportunities. I think he's fallen in love with Vermont."

"And with the young lady as well?"

"Oh, Mr. O'Leary, wouldn't that be nice? I just hope she's a good person."

"Yes, let's hope so. You go right ahead, Mrs. Murphy. Mike and I were talking about that order you just brought in. It seems we have no one to serve it on, now that your brother-in-law has flown the coop. We thought he might have made his secretary an officer of his professional corporation."

"Why would he make his secretary an officer?"

"Solo practitioners often do. It's just for the convenience of having someone around to sign things when they're unavailable. Unfortunately, his secretary says he didn't, so we have no one to serve with the order, even if we get it signed."

"Will that hurt our case, Mr. O'Leary?"

"It doesn't help. One of our concerns is what Chris might do with the estate funds if he has financial problems, and disappearing the way he has certainly can't inspire confidence in any of his clients who might be trying to reach him. His fee income will dry up fast when they can't even get in touch with him. What we'd like to do is lock up the estate assets before he has a chance to do anything with them. Unfortunately, we don't have the information we'd be required to provide to the court in order for it to issue an order directing whatever financial institution holds the estate account to freeze it. In other words, we don't know where the money is."

"But Frank wanted Hanny to have that money, not my brother-in-law."

"I know. That's why we need to find the money. So we can protect it. Now you go to lunch. We'll figure something out."

Mrs. Murphy left the room, dabbing her eyes with a handkerchief as she went.

"I feel sorry for her, Mike, but what else can we do? Her brother-in-law is a bad apple. I just hope he hasn't taken a powder with her son's inheritance."

"We'll get him, Tim, we'll get him."

"Let's hope. So, you mentioned earlier that something interesting happened yesterday. What was it?"

"Well first of all, we've got a new tenant for Max Karraten's office next door. An accountant. Her lease starts the first of the month, but she's supposed to come by this morning to take some measurements."

"How long is the lease?"

"Just a year. Considering how busy we've been, I was thinking we might want to bring in another lawyer before much longer, and maybe another secretary. If that happens, we'll need more space."

"Yeah. In the meantime, it'll be nice to have some rent coming in."

"Anyway, that's only part of the story, so back to the missing Mr. Murphy. You had said Marge has been having trouble tracking him down?"

"It's all dead ends so far. Apparently, he's a bachelor, so no wife or kids for us to talk to. He belongs to a couple of local clubs—Rotary, the Elks Lodge, and so on, but it sounds like he's not active with any of them. Goes to the Lodge for lunch now and then, but not lately, and he doesn't seem to have any close friends there. He has all his mail sent to his office, and the junk mail is overflowing the mailbox outside his house. His neighbors, those who would talk, don't know him very well, and no one has seen him around lately."

"So, nothing."

"Unfortunately, but she'll keep trying."

"I've been holding out on you the past few minutes, because I wanted hear what you had first. This new tenant, her name is Carolyn Kerwick."

"What about her?"

"She was renting space in a lawyer's office until a few weeks ago, but he suddenly told her he was cancelling his own lease, so she'd have to leave. He gave her thirty days' notice to move out. Guess who he is?"

"How would I know?"

"Well, it just so happens he's our friend Chris Murphy."

"You're kidding."

"Would I kid about something like that? Sorry, my man, but it looks like our friend Chris has travel plans."

"Am I interrupting?'

An attractive young woman was standing in the doorway to Tim's office.

35

"WELL, HI, CAROLYN. Come right in. Tim and I were just talking about you. Tim, this is our new tenant, Carolyn Kerwick. Miss Kerwick, meet my partner, Tim O'Leary."

Tim stood.

"Nice to meet you, Miss Kerwick. Mike was just telling me you're about to become our neighbor."

"Yes, and first names work for me. May I call you Tim?"

"Yes, please do. I also hear you were working out of Chris Murphy's office until now."

"Yes, I was, but he's closing his office, so I have to leave. It was awfully short notice. I'm lucky I learned about your space."

"So are we. Did you hear about what happened to our previous tenant?"

"Yes, I did. Very sad."

"It was. But your taking the space will help his family, who won't be responsible for making payments on the rest of his lease now. In any case, could we talk to you for a few minutes before you go next door to take your measurements?"

"Sure."

They went out to the reception area and sat down.

"Carolyn, I told Tim what you said about Chris Murphy, but I didn't have a chance to tell him all of it," Mike said. "Would you mind if we go over it again?"

"Not at all."

"Okay. As I understand it, this happened sort of suddenly."

"Yes, it did. He just walked in a couple of weeks ago and told me he had exercised an option to cancel his lease, effective October thirty-first, and that I would have to leave. I was basically a month-to-month tenant, so I really had no grounds to object, but I still thought he was being very inconsiderate. Anyway, I heard him fussing around with some paperwork for a few hours, and then he left. He never came back."

"You mean that day?" Tim said.

"No, I mean never. I haven't seen him since."

"What about his secretary? Did she give you any indication where he might be?"

"No, she actually seemed more confused than I was."

"What about his files?"

"That's hard to say. He had some file cabinets, but I didn't look inside or anything. He may have taken a few papers with him that day, but no more than a briefcase full, I would think, and I haven't seen a moving van pulling up. My guess is whatever files he had would still be in the file cabinets."

"Did he ever talk to you about matters he was handling?"

"Not really. To tell you the truth, we mostly kept to ourselves. I spoke to his secretary more than I spoke to him. She was very nice about answering my phone and doing a little typing for me when she had time. I paid her for that, of course."

"Did he ever mention the Murphy estate to you?"

"No, but I heard him yelling something about his 'stupid sister-in-law and her numbskull of a son' once. It was the day a process server showed up at the office with papers to serve on him."

"How did you know it was a process server?"

"Well, I think it was. I was returning from the ladies' room down the hall, and a man asked me which office was Mr. Murphy's. He said he had some papers for him. I showed him our office door and went in after him. It was just a few minutes later, right after I sat down at my desk in the other room, that I heard Chris yelling."

"Did Chris tell you anything about what had happened?"

"Nothing. The next time he spoke to me was a few days later, when he gave me my thirty days' notice. Then he was gone."

"Oh, man, this gets stranger all the time," Mike said. "Tim, did you have any other questions?"

"Not at the moment. Thanks, Carolyn, and welcome to the building. We hope you like it here. Let us know if you need anything."

"Will do, Tim."

36

TWENTY MINUTES LATER, Mrs. Murphy returned from lunch with Hannibal in tow.

Tim greeted them from the couch, where he and Mike were still sitting.

"Hey, Hanny, over here! How are you? Your mom tells me you're going back up to Vermont tomorrow."

"Yeah, by bus. It's a long ride, but it should be beautiful with the leaves changing. Margaret says early October is peak season in northern Vermont."

"So I understand. I wish I could join you. I heard you'll be seeing Margaret while you're there."

"I will. We've talked a few times on the phone since I came back to New York, and we agreed to get together the next time I came to Jay."

"Glad to hear it. On a less positive note, I suppose your mom told you we're having some trouble finding your uncle Chris."

"She did. He can act very strange sometimes. Will it be a problem if you can't find him?"

"Yes and no. The bigger problem is finding out where

he's put your father's estate assets."

"Doesn't he have a secretary? Why don't you ask her?"

Tim looked at Mike, who looked at Hanny, and then back at Tim.

"Why didn't we think of that, Tim? It's so obvious. We'll make you a lawyer, yet, Hanny."

Hanny blanched.

"Thanks, but I don't think that's for me, Mike."

Tim laughed.

"He's just kidding, Hanny, but you know, now that I think about it—"

Hanny looked from one to the other nervously, then realized they were teasing him, and breathed an exaggerated sigh of relief

"Okay, back to Hanny's idea, Mike. Carolyn Kerwick said the secretary was clueless as to what was going on. She can't be too happy with Chris right now. She must be very hurt, to say nothing about being worried about where her next paycheck is coming from. I think she'd be sympathetic to Hanny's plight, given the obvious parallels to her own financial concerns. She may very well be willing to share that information with us"

"One problem though," Mike said. "It might be an ethical violation for us to approach an adversary's staff member for information about a pending litigation. That would be like your buddy Marty Zanger calling Mrs. Murphy and asking her which item your client Alfie Casey was going to pick if he won the coin toss—the one Marty flipped—in poor Alfie's battle with his sister Bridget over their mother's treasures. Goodbye red bicycle, Alfie! Mrs. Murphy blew your cover!"

Tim grimaced.

"You're right, Mike, but I bet she knows a lot. There must have been calls, letters, bank statements, tax returns, and everything else a secretary would have seen and heard. I wish we could speak to her."

"Let's let the court decide, Tim. There's a man's estate involved here, an estate that he wanted to go to his son. Give me that draft order. Let's make some changes. I'll need the name of Chris Murphy's secretary, and a few other things. Carolyn Kerwick can fill me in there."

Mike called out to Mrs. Murphy, who had returned to her desk.

"Mrs. Murphy, could you come over here. I might have to ask you to stay a little late tonight. Hanny, have a nice time in Vermont, but stay in touch, okay? We may need you before this is over."

"Okay. I'll let my mom know where I'm staying once I get up there. Thank you both for helping me."

37

A COURT-ORDERED SUBPOENA was signed the next day by the acting Surrogate, but with modifications. Instead of directing Chris Murphy's secretary to turn over the estate records to Tim's firm, the subpoena directed her to bring the file to the courthouse for examination by the judge. Any privileged information, such as communications between Murphy and his clients, would be removed from the file before it was made available to Mike and Tim for their inspection. Later, if necessary, the attorneys could make a further application to the court for an order directing the secretary to submit to a deposition regarding the handling of the estate by her office.

Mike laughed off the suggestion that the file might contain confidential communications between Chris Murphy and a client.

"The only 'client' is Murphy himself," he said.

Of greater concern was the possibility that the court might drag its feet in reviewing the files, giving Murphy time to make off with the estate assets, assuming he hadn't done so already.

Mike served the subpoena himself, traveling straight to

Chris Murphy's office after picking up a copy from the courthouse. He called Carolyn Kerwick first, to make sure Murphy's secretary was in, and asked Carolyn to try to stall her if it looked like she might be planning to leave before he got there.

Chris Murphy's secretary was a woman in her mid-forties, whose name was Mandy Schwartz. She was hardworking, pleasant, and furious at Murphy, which became apparent as soon as Mike arrived. He held the papers out to her, and as she read the name of the estate on the top page, she jumped up from her desk and nearly screamed at him.

"This has to do with his brother's estate? His personal cash cow? Tell him his broker wants a current certificate of his appointment before they'll transfer the estate account. A paycheck for me might help pay the cab fare, so I can go over to the courthouse to pick one up. And while you're at it—"

"Whoa, easy! I'm just here to serve a court-ordered subpoena."

"Well, I'm not here to take it. You'll have to find that creep yourself if you want to serve him with anything. And when you do, you can tell him that I quit! I quit! Do you hear me? I ..."

Mandy had exhausted her shallow reservoir of aggressiveness. She started to sob, and slumped back into her chair.

Mike gently laid the subpoena on her desk. As he turned to go, Carolyn Kerwick hurried into the room.

"Mandy, don't cry," she said. "This is just Mike Green from the office I told you about. They're trying to help Mrs. Murphy and her son. Why don't we look at these papers? Mike, could you stay for a minute? Maybe you could explain why you're here."

"Sure, Carolyn. Miss Schwartz, my name is Mike Green. I'm a lawyer from the office that has been trying to get your boss to wind up his brother's estate and turn over the assets to his nephew."

"Good luck with that," Mandy said, trying to collect herself.

"So far, we haven't been getting much cooperation," Mike said. "as you seem to know, and now it looks like your boss has disappeared. We're all very concerned, particularly since we don't even know where the money is. The judge has agreed that the situation is serious enough that any documents or information you might have regarding the estate should be turned over to the court. This subpoena directs you to do that."

"Directs me?"

"Yes. We assumed you would be familiar with the estate, given your employment here."

"What type of information?"

"Where the estate accounts are maintained. The person Mr. Murphy deals with at the bank or brokerage firm where the accounts are located. Statements for those accounts, correspondence, anything that might help us get control over the assets before something tragic occurs."

"You mean like Chris making off with the money?"

"Yes."

"He hasn't done that yet, at least as far as I know. I guess he was trying to do something with the account, though, given that request for a certificate I yelled at you about. Sorry."

"Not a problem. It's fine. I think we're all a little upset about this. Where was he going to transfer the estate account?"

"He didn't tell me. His broker calling and asking for the certificate was the first I heard about it."

"So, it hasn't been moved yet?"

"I don't think so."

"Why did you refer to the estate as his 'cash cow' before?"

"Just because that's what it is. He's constantly telling me to draw checks to him for his legal fees and his trustee's commissions."

"You mean his executor's commissions?"

"No, he took all of those a long time ago."

"But he's not the trustee. Mrs. Murphy is."

"I know, but he said he's a 'de facto' trustee, because she's incapable of doing the job."

"Oh, boy. This thing sounds worse all the time. Well, could you put the files together? I'll give you a ride over to the Surrogate's Court when you're ready."

38

FORTUNATELY, THE COURT made short work of its examination of the files to see if any privileged information had to be protected from disclosure. As Mike had predicted, the court found none, so he and Tim were notified that they were free to review the documents in their entirety at the courthouse. Tim, being more familiar with the background, took on this responsibility.

The files were fairly complete, but not voluminous. Essentially, they reflected the probate of the Will, the appointment of both the executor and the trustee, and the collection and investment of the proceeds of the lawsuit brought with respect to the accident that took Hanny's father's life. There were virtually no other assets. Payments had been made for estate and income taxes, legal fees, and commissions, but not much else. The investments were fairly routine, at least initially, but as time passed, that changed dramatically.

With his extensive professional experience, Tim knew that estate assets should be liquidated quickly, as had happened here by way of the successful completion of the lawsuit and the collection of the cash settlement proceeds. After receiving these funds as executor, Chris Murphy did deposit them in interest-bearing estate accounts, while paying out the monies needed to meet the estate's financial obligations.

Over time, however, a new pattern began to develop. Instead of continuing to keep the funds invested on a short-term basis, in interest-bearing bank accounts or government bonds, so as to preserve them until they could be distributed to the beneficiary, Chris had reversed course. In a fairly short period of time, he had started moving aggressively into stocks, and recently, into speculative investments such as puts and calls. Of late, he had even done some of the investing on margin, in effect borrowing money to buy more of these types of investments. Knowing his brother's son was missing, and believing he had little to fear from his ex-sister-in-law, Murphy had obviously seen an opportunity to launch a profitable investment fund, with himself at the helm.

Although it was inappropriate for an executor to treat an estate account as an investment account, the securities initially purchased were "blue chip" stocks, for the most part, and under ordinary circumstances might not have been a major concern. They were largely the currently popular tech and entertainment stocks, such as Texas Instruments and Disney, which he could have liquidated quickly to prepare for final distribution to Hanny.

These more recent developments in the account, however, were very concerning. Major purchases of the same securities had been made on margin in the last month, and the account's margin debt now approached half of its total value. The derivative investments—the puts and calls—added to Tim's unease. Chris was obviously looking for a big score, and showed a willingness to take major risks to achieve it.

Once he had finished making notes, Tim went out in the hallway to call Mike, so he could fill him in on what he had learned. He waited more than ten minutes for one of the phone booths to open up, before discovering he didn't have the change needed to make the call.

Cursing himself for not thinking ahead, he left the booth and walked down the street to retrieve his car from the parking garage. One of these days they'd perfect those new portable phones, he thought to himself. In the meantime, Nokia's twenty-one pound "made for your car" device didn't exactly fit in your pocket. He had heard of a Motorola version that weighed only two pounds, but cost $4,000, which was pretty pricey just to make a few telephone calls.

Tim reached the garage, paid the attendant, and decided it might be a good time to speak with Mandy Schwartz. He drove off, hoping to catch her before she left Chris Murphy's office for the day. Mike had described what she looked like, and Tim saw a woman meeting that description coming out of the building as he pulled up to the curb twenty minutes later. Rolling down the passenger side window, he leaned over and called out to her.

"Miss Schwartz? Miss Schwartz, could I impose on you for a few minutes?"

She stopped, startled.

"Miss Schwartz, I'm Mike Green's partner, Tim O'Leary. You met Mike when he served you with papers in the Murphy estate. We're the attorneys for Madeline Murphy and her son Hannibal."

"I haven't been paid in weeks," she said, her voice clipped. "I don't see why I should work overtime."

She started walking away.

Tim killed the engine, jumped out of the car and hurried to catch up to her.

"Miss Schwartz," he said, "I know that what's been going on is very unfair to you, but I'm trying to help someone who's also been hurt by Chris Murphy."

She glanced at him, but kept moving.

"I think you can sympathize with that. He's just a young kid," Tim said. "He's lost his father, and now he stands to lose everything his father wanted him to have. Would you at least let me walk along with you, so I can ask a few questions?"

"Do whatever you want. I don't own the sidewalk. But I'm getting on my bus in three blocks, and I'm not going to miss it."

She walked faster.

Tim, hurrying to keep pace, tried to get to the point.

"Miss Schwartz, I've just finished reviewing the files you turned over to the Surrogate's Court. It looks like Chris Murphy has been buying stocks on margin in the estate account, and making other speculative investments as well. He really shouldn't be doing that. It's risky enough for anyone, but to do it with estate money is downright reckless. Did he ever discuss that with you?"

"Discuss?" She smirked. "Not his style. I asked him about it when I saw the first brokerage trade confirmation that showed loans. I didn't even know what 'margin' meant. I thought it was the space between the side of a page and the typed text. He just said it wasn't my concern, that it was a shrewd way to take advantage of the booming stock market. You could get 'more for your money,' he said, and that I should do it myself with my 'savings.' Ha! That was a laugh. He paid me barely enough to pay for my rent and my groceries."

She continued walking.

"Did he say why he had started doing it all of a sudden, after so many months of just investing the estate account in stocks and bonds?"

"He just said the market was so good it would be remiss of him not to take advantage of the opportunity to increase the 'blue chip portfolio' he was managing."

"Did he ever tell you when he was planning to distribute the investments to his nephew?"

"Just the opposite. He said he'd have to hold onto them indefinitely, that the 'boy' was too immature and 'whacked out' to be able to handle that much money himself, and that he owed it to his late brother to 'protect and preserve' the family's 'nest egg.'"

"The family's or his nephew's?"

"The family's. Here's my stop. I have to go."

An MTA bus had just pulled to the curb, and people were starting to board.

"One other thing before you go, Miss Schwartz. Do you recall anything happening that might have led Mr. Murphy to start buying stocks on margin?"

"Oh, that one's easy. It was right after you phoned him to say young Hannibal had been found, and that you wanted to discuss winding up the estate."

She stepped onto the bus, and the door closed behind her.

39

TIM KNEW THE SITUATION was critical. Something had to be done, and done quickly, before the estate assets vanished. The courts were notoriously slow. The famous quote "the wheels of justice turn slowly, but grind exceedingly fine" described the system more often than not. Nevertheless, he had no other option.

So, the following morning, instead of going to the office, he drove to the Bronx County courthouse, entered the building and took the elevator to Surrogate's Court offices. Remembering that it was Constance Logan of the court's law department who had been directed to check with Chris Murphy's office the day he failed to appear on the call of the calendar, Tim asked the receptionist if he could speak to her.

A short time later, Miss Logan stepped out and invited Tim to join her in her office. Offering him a seat, she told him one of the interns had reviewed the subpoenaed file for privileged information. Having found none, the intern had been instructed to call Tim's office to let him know he could come in and look through the file. Logan herself had been tied up on another matter, and hadn't seen the file herself yet, but planned on doing so today. She asked Tim if he had done so.

He told her he had, and he described what was in the file, as well as what he had learned from his conversation with Mandy Schwartz.

Logan was an experienced court attorney, but she still expressed surprise at what she was hearing.

"Where has he gone?"

"No one knows, Miss Logan. Not his secretary, not the accountant who rents office space in his suite, no one. We've learned that he's single, and we haven't been able to find any close friends. Basically, he's a mystery man.

"We have also learned that he was trying to move the estate brokerage account out of New York, but we got lucky there. Given the length of time since he was appointed executor, the firm where the estate account is located asked for a current certification that his appointment is still in force. His broker hadn't realized that would be necessary when he took Murphy's transfer instructions. Then he found out, but when he called Murphy's office to tell him, Murphy was gone."

"Do you know where the transfer was supposed to go?"

"No. Maybe someplace in Arizona."

"Arizona? Not the Cayman Islands, or Monaco, or someplace exotic like that?"

"His secretary told my partner that he bought a timeshare in Arizona last year. She doesn't know the address, but she heard him talking about it on the phone one day."

"Which brokerage handles the estate account?"

"EF Hutton."

"Didn't they have some trouble recently?"

"Loads. A check kiting scandal in the Northeast, a money laundering scandal up in Rhode Island, you name it. An old-line firm that developed some bad habits."

"And they allow estate accounts to be invested on margin?"

"Apparently so."

"All right, I think I've heard enough. I'm going to speak to Lee Holtzman about getting an emergency order freezing the account so it can't be transferred, and revoking Mr. Murphy's appointment as executor. At least that will maintain the status quo, but the court isn't going to make investment decisions. We'll need a new executor in place to do that. Is a successor executor named in the Will?"

"There isn't. The only fiduciaries appointed were Christopher Murphy, who was named executor, and our client Madeline Murphy, who was named trustee for her son's trust."

"Is she the surviving spouse?"

"No. They were divorced."

"The trust is for the son?"

"That's right."

"Any other children?"

"No. Only the one."

"Is he a minor?"

"No. He's twenty-four. He'll be twenty-five in a several weeks. That's when the trust ends."

"Okay, so we have one distributee, and he also happens to be the sole beneficiary, at least if he hangs in there a little while longer. There's our successor. If he's competent and willing, we'll make him administrator c.t.a. and we can get this thing under control. Questions?"

The rapidity of Logan's analysis, and her decisiveness in proposing a solution, stunned Tim. He wasn't used to this kind of swift justice in the courts in the five boroughs, but he certainly wasn't going to complain. The only problem he foresaw was Hanny's availability. Hoping Hanny hadn't ventured out on another lengthy trek in the New England wilderness, he stifled his concerns, and responded.

"Only one, Miss Logan, can we—"

She cut him off.

"Call me Connie. It takes less time. I assume I can call you Tim. What's your question?"

"Should we submit an order revoking Chris Murphy's letters? If so, how will we serve him with notice when we don't know where he is?"

"No need. This court has an obligation to protect the estates of our deceased citizens and their families. Sometimes we must exercise our powers without the procedural delays that could undermine the performance of that function. This is obviously such a time."

"I couldn't agree more, Connie. Do we need to worry about any objection from Mr. Murphy later, however, that he had no opportunity to be heard?"

"The executor has ignored an order to appear and show cause why he shouldn't be compelled to account," she said. "He has apparently left the jurisdiction without notice, and he has attempted to remove the estate assets from the state, in clear violation of the rules governing his office. Speculation with those assets is per se objectionable. We're not going to wait for his return for an explanation. There's too much at stake. The court will issue an order revoking his appointment today."

"I appreciate your moving so expeditiously," Tim said. "Can anything else be done to ensure the funds remain in place, before the son is in place as administrator c.t.a.?"

"The order will also restrain EF Hutton from taking any action with regard to the estate account until a successor fiduciary is appointed. I want you to serve a copy of the order on them when you leave here. And I want you to bring young Mr. Murphy back as soon as possible, so we can get him appointed to take over the administration of his father's estate. I'll be right back."

Miss Logan stood and walked out of the room, leaving Tim somewhat breathless. Courts didn't usually act this way. Slow and slower was the standard. Maybe Connie Logan represented a different future. He hoped so.

Twenty minutes later, she returned.

"I spoke with Lee Holtzman. He's arranging to have the order signed as soon as I get it typed up. You can go back to your office, and we'll give you a call when the it's ready. Then you can pick up a certified copy and serve it on an officer of EF Hutton. That will prevent any transfer of the account until we get a new fiduciary in place. We'll wait for you to let us know when the son is ready to qualify as administrator c.t.a. That's all we can do for now. Have a good day."

40

MIKE WAS IMPRESSED.

"You mean they didn't tell you to make a motion, start a new proceeding, make a contribution to Lee Holtzman's election campaign, nothing?" Mike said.

"Very funny. No, no, and definitely no. Besides, I don't think Holtzman has much to worry about in November. His two opponents in the Democratic primary got bounced for not getting enough signatures on their petitions. They sued and got back on the ballot, but he beat them both, anyway. Now all he's got to do is beat a Republican in the general election. That should be no problem. Republicans never win anything in the Bronx. I'll tell you something, though, if this Connie Logan is ever looking for a job, I'd be the first on line to hire her."

"You and me both, Tim. We're getting awfully busy. I think we're going to have to bring in another lawyer one of these days. So, anyway, what's the basis for removing Murphy without notice?"

"Chris could have been summarily removed under either of the first two paragraphs of Section 719 of the SCPA, and half of paragraph ten as well. Three strikes and he's out. But for the court to actually do it on the spot, like she did, was a stunner. I was shocked."

The telephone rang.

"Mr. O'Leary, it's the Bronx County Surrogate's Court," Mrs. Murphy called out.

Tim picked up the phone.

"Tim O'Leary … Yes, Miss Logan, I mean Connie, yes. Thanks. I'll come over now."

Tim got up from his desk, told Mrs. Murphy he was on his way to court, and left. A half hour later, he walked out of the Bronx County Courthouse smiling, order in hand. Getting back into his car, he saw a ticket on the windshield, and realized there was a sign he'd failed to notice earlier, which prohibited parking of non-official vehicles in the space he had taken. Too happy about the court's order to care, he grabbed the ticket, stuffed it in his pocket, checked a map for directions, and started toward the EF Hutton office where Chris Murphy maintained the estate account. Despite a fair amount of traffic, he managed to get to the office well before closing time. Unable to find a legal parking spot, he pulled into a parking garage a block away, left his car there, and walked to the office.

A man was sitting at a desk in a modest cubicle near the entrance to the office. His appearance was unremarkable. He looked to be in his early fifties, with thinning gray hair and a slightly ruddy complexion. The nameplate on his desk identified him as Halbert Baker, Assistant Vice President. Recognizing the name from the account statements Mandy Schwartz had produced, Tim approached him.

"Mr. Baker?"

Baker looked up.

"Yes? Can I help you?"

"My name is Tim O'Leary. I'm here to serve EF Hutton with a court order. I see from your nameplate that you're an officer of the corporation, so I am now serving the order on you."

He handed the paper to Baker, who looked down at it as he began to rise. Then he sat back down.

"The Murphy estate. I can't say I'm surprised. Let's hope you're not too late."

"Too late? What do you mean by that?"

"Chris Murphy called three days ago to ask why the estate account hadn't been transferred. He said he'd been away on a business trip. He said he'd been calling our Scottsdale office over and over to see if they'd received the estate account yet. The answer was always no, not yet. Finally, he called me, like I just said. I told him I had left a message at his office, but he obviously hadn't heard about it, so I explained what we needed."

"How did he react?" Tim said.

"He hung up, and then called back a few minutes later, really pissed off," Baker said. "Sounded like he'd called his office and chewed out his secretary for not going over to the courthouse for the certificate we needed. I think they had words, and she refused to help him. He told me I should send someone over to the court to get it, but I told him I had no authority to do that. Then he hung up on me again."

"A class act," Tim said.

"There's more," Baker said. "The day before yesterday, Chris showed up here with an updated certificate from the court, proving he was still the executor. He said he'd had to fly into town so he could get it. He seemed really annoyed about the delay in our transferring the estate account, calling our compliance department's request for current documentation 'typical bureaucratic bullshit,' to use his words. Then he muttered something about filing a complaint with the Securities and Exchange Commission if we didn't get this thing done 'pronto.'"

"Oh, lord! You've got to stop that transfer!"

"I'll do what I can. Sit down, Mr. O'Leary. I'll be right back."

Tim sat, but couldn't stay sitting. He got up and fretfully

paced back and forth while he waited for Baker to return.

Fifteen minutes later, Baker was back.

"I spoke to my manager. He's on the phone with our transfer department. He said he'd buzz me as soon as he has an answer. You're making me nervous, Mr. O'Leary. Why don't you take your seat and we can wait together."

Tim sat. and asked, "When Chris Murphy brought the updated documentation, did he tell you where he's been?"

"Just the same thing about a business trip. He didn't say to where, or for what. Just that we'd better get this done, or 'heads will roll,' as he put it. Then he was gone. What's this all about, anyway?"

Tim summarized the recent developments as clearly as he could, trying his best to impress Baker with the urgency of the situation. He suspected that if the account had been transferred, it wouldn't stay in Arizona for very long.

The intercom on Baker's desk hummed. He pressed a button on the device.

"Yes, boss?"

41

BAKER RETURNED THE PHONE to its cradle and looked up.

"We might have gotten lucky, Mr. O'Leary. Some kid in operations, an intern from one of the law schools, told a supervisor the account shouldn't be moved out of state without prior court permission, and the posting of a bond. Something about the 'SCPA,' whatever that is, but it sounded like a statute. So, the supervisor bounced it off legal, which always takes its time getting things done. He was waiting for them to get back to him, but Scottsdale was going berserk. They'd love to get the account, of course, just like I'd like to keep it. I think the kid's supervisor was about to give in when you showed up with your court order. I told my manager. He told legal. They told operations. End of story. The account stays here. I think I owe you a drink."

Tim realized he had been holding his breath. He exhaled with relief.

"No need, Mr. Baker. Buy one for that intern instead. In fact, let's both buy him one. Or two."

"Her, Mr. O'Leary, he's a she."

"Wow, I must be getting old, but I should have known.

First Connie Logan and now this. Thank God for women. I'll have to tell Marge."

"Who's that?"

"My wife. She's a private investigator. Another pioneer."

"Well, good for her. So now who's going to handle the estate account? Will there be a new executor?"

"Yes. Well, actually an 'administrator c.t.a.' It's really the same thing, but it's the term used for the person who's in charge when there's a vacancy, and when there's no alternate executor named in the Will."

"Do you know who it's going to be?"

"Yes, the son. He's out of town right now, visiting his girlfriend, among other things, but I'll get in touch with him as soon as I can, so we can get the procedure going."

"You might want to hurry. There're puts, calls, margin purchases, everything under the sun going on in that account. Somebody needs to be in a position to give instructions real soon."

"Can't you just sell everything and put it in cash? The estate will be wound up very quickly, as soon as we have a new fiduciary in place."

"Sorry, we don't have trading authority. We just carry out orders."

"Understood. Is there a phone I can use? I'd like to call my office, and see if my secretary knows where young Mr. Murphy can be reached right now."

Baker pointed to the telephone on his desk. "Be my guest," Baker said. "I need to use the john, anyway."

Tim realized he'd been avoiding referring to Hanny by name today. He didn't have time for more jokes about Hannibal and his elephants. He picked up the phone and dialed the office.

"Mrs. Murphy? Good. I'm glad I caught you. Have you heard from your son? The court issued an order removing Chris from office and freezing the estate account, but we need to have Hanny appointed as administrator so we can unwind those risky investments Chris has been making."

He paused for a moment, then frowned.

"Did he tell you when he'd be back?"

Tim reached for a calendar on Baker's desk and looked at the dates.

"Monday? Four days from now? It's important that I speak to him. The court will appoint him to take over the administration of the estate, but he has to sign some papers first."

He paused again, frowning as he listened.

Yes, I know it's peak season and he loves it up there, and that he has a girlfriend, and ... a job? Where?"

He hesitated for a moment, then made a decision.

"All right, Mrs. Murphy. This is important. I'm going to need you to type some papers for me in the morning. Then I'll drive up there over the weekend and have him sign them when he gets back."

He hung up the phone and looked up. Baker had returned, and was staring at him.

"Trouble?"

"You could say that, Mr. Baker. That was my guy's mother. She says he spoke to our part-time secretary and told her to tell his mother that he'd be away for a few days, and apparently out of touch. He won't return to civilization until Monday morning."

"Civilization? You mean New York?"

"No, I mean Vermont."

"We have an office in Burlington. Is that where he lives?"

"Have you ever heard of a place by the name of Danby Four Corners?"

Baker laughed.

"Can't say I have. I don't think we have an office there."

Tim tried to force a smile, without success.

"I wish I could laugh too, but this estate could go downhill fast while we're waiting for him to make his way back to something called the Stoney House Center."

Baker chuckled.

"What else did your part-timer tell her?"

"That Hannibal would call her when he arrived."

"Hah! Did his mother buy all that? Or the part-timer? Danby's four daughters? Stoney House? Some guy named Hannibal would call her? Next thing we'll hear is that Hannibal's there because he decided to cross the Green Mountains instead of the Alps this time. C'mon. Enough's enough. Give the guy a break. You said it yourself just a few minutes ago. He's got a girlfriend up there. Let him enjoy a few days without checking in with his mother. Let's pack up. Market's closed. Time for me to shut down for the night."

Tim started to explain about Hanny's name, then thought better of it.

"Okay, Mr. Baker. Joke's on her, I guess. Thanks for your help. I'll be in touch as soon as we have an administrator in place. Have a good evening."

"You too, Mr. O'Leary. I'll just saddle up my elephant and be on my way."

He removed a jacket from the back of his chair and walked toward the office door, still chuckling.

Tim shrugged resignedly and followed.

42

"SO, YOU'RE GOING UP THERE?"

"I have to, Marge. If I don't catch Hanny at this Stoney House place when he gets back, he's liable to turn around and disappear with another group for a week or two. He loves that stuff, and he doesn't know what's been going on in his father's estate."

"True. Let's have some dinner, and then we can help Katie with her lines for the school play."

"The play? That's not until Christmas time, is it? How many lines does she have?"

"A couple, I think."

"I thought she just had to say she feels fine?"

"There are a few more. Mostly about a flower she won at school, but the line about not having a temperature is the one she's having trouble with."

"It doesn't sound too hard. What's the problem?"

"Her sister Janie says Zuzu doesn't have a smitch of temperature. She wants to know what a 'smitch' is. Katie thinks it's like a 'snitch,' someone who tells on someone else. 'Why would somebody snitch on the temperature,

Mommy?' she asked me."

"Well, that's fair enough. What is a 'smitch,' anyway?"

"For one thing, it's supposed to be a 'smidge,' but Janie pronounces it 'smitch.' I think smidge is short for 'smidgen,' or a very small amount."

"So why doesn't Janie just say, 'not a speck,' or 'not a shred,' or 'not a bit,' or—"

Marge sighed.

"Because that's not what she said in the movie."

"Who's going to know?"

"Who's going to know? Everyone, Tim, everyone. I don't know a single person who hasn't seen that movie. A lot of people have watched it more than once, many times more than once. It's so popular, especially around Christmas time … Wait a second, don't tell me you've never seen *It's A Wonderful Life*."

"Actually, no. What's it about?"

"Oh my gosh. You really don't know, do you? It's just the perfect Christmas story. About someone who doesn't realize how much he's done for so many people, who thinks he's a loser, who has no idea how many people love him, how many people would do anything for him, and who finally get the chance. You know what I'm going to do? I'm going to take you to see it the next time it comes to a movie theater around here."

"All right, but what about Katie? How can we get her not to worry about her sister saying stitch? I mean smitch? Or midge, or whatever it is? And what about her own lines?"

"Oh, I think she'll be fine with them. She likes the part where Zuzu is talking to her daddy about the flower she won at school, and the part where she runs out of her room after she hears the other kids shouting, 'Merry Christmas, daddy!' right near the end, and then she happily says 'Daddy!' too. The thing she likes the most, though, is at the very end, when Zuzu tells her daddy that the teacher told the kids in her class at school that every time a bell rings, an angel gets his wings."

"That's in the movie, too?"

"Yes, it is. You have got to see that movie. But, first, why don't you go tell the kids it's time for dinner?"

Tim left the kitchen, and was back in a few minutes with Timmy and Katie. He helped Katie climb into her seat, where he'd placed a telephone book for a little extra elevation.

As soon as they began to eat, Timmy, a newly-minted teenager as of his recently celebrated thirteenth birthday earlier that year, looked at Tim with a grin on his face.

"Did you hear that Katie is playing a crow and a squirrel in the high school play?"

Katie threw a carrot at him.

"I am not, Timmy. I'm playing zoo zoo."

"That's where those animals are, aren't they?"

"Not that kind of zoo. The kind that's a little girl, like me."

"I know. That's why you're playing a crow and a squirrel. I didn't think they had those kinds of animals there. At least not in the cages."

"Mom, tell him to stop."

"Yes, Timmy, leave Katie alone. Don't be mean."

Tim was still trying to figure out this Wonderful Life thing. Now he was really confused.

"You mean there are squirrels and crows in this movie you were telling me about, Marge? Are there scenes in a park or something?"

"No, they're in the bank, or in Uncle Billy's house."

"Squirrels and crows in a bank?"

"Uncle Billy works at the bank. He's sort of eccentric. He brings his pet crow to work with him."

Timmy chimed in.

"Maybe they can stay in Katie's room while she's getting ready for the play."

Katie screeched and threw a spoon at her brother. He caught it in midair and held it out to her.

"Better hang on to this, little sister, you'll need it to feed your new pets."

"Mom! I said tell him to stop."

Tim was still confused, but he figured it was time for him to get involved.

"Yes, Timmy, leave her alone. Can't you see you're upsetting your little sister? Don't worry, sweetie, he's only teasing you. All you have to do in the play is talk to your daddy, right, mommy? She doesn't have to play with squirrels or crows or anything like that."

Marge didn't respond at first.

"Right?" he added hopefully.

"You know what, Tim? I think it might be fun for both of you if you took Timmy to Vermont with you on Sunday. He's never been there, and school is closed on Monday for Columbus Day. Would you like that, Timmy?"

Timmy brightened. This was a surprise, a good one.

"Yeah. I've never been anywhere. Do they have skiing up there yet?"

Tim laughed.

"I hope not, Timmy. This is apple picking and leaf peeping season."

"So, when do they start skiing?"

"From what I hear, Killington likes to open for Thanksgiving, but that's a little early. Most areas just hope they'll get enough snow to bring the skiers up for Christmas week. Maybe we can try it this winter, but for now it should be beautiful up there with the leaves turning, and everything crisp and clean. I know you'll like it."

43

MILE AFTER MILE of gorgeous autumn foliage lined both sides of the Taconic Parkway, presenting an idyllic panorama disrupted only now and then by a state trooper's vehicle emerging from its hiding place to nail another speeder. In no hurry himself, Tim stayed within a few miles of the fifty-five mile per hour speed limit as other drivers blew past him, taking their chances. A few deer grazed here and there by the roadside, and the changing leaves blazed with increasing splendor as the car traveled north.

Their route, which a friend of Tim's had suggested, avoided the interstates in favor of a more direct and scenic path. The driving would be a bit slower, but the route forty miles shorter, and his friend promised it would cut their overall travel time. This, he said, was of course contingent on Tim respecting the Taconic's speed limit so as to avoid getting pulled over. Sound advice, Tim thought, as he watched another police cruiser emerge from behind a grove of trees and race after a sedan that had just passed him doing about seventy.

"Hey, dad, why don't we go faster now? That cop's busy with the guy who just passed us."

Tim was tempted. After all, what Timmy said made sense, so he started to accelerate. Just then, the road curved, and they saw yet another police cruiser, parked on the grass off the right side of the road.

"Uh oh, better skip it, dad."

"Agreed."

Tim lifted his foot off the gas pedal, and as he did, a yellow Corvette roared past them. Apparently seeing the police cruiser at the last minute, the driver braked, although he still looked like he was doing at least seventy as he went by. To their surprise, the cruiser didn't move.

"Wow, the cop must not have been paying attention, dad. That guy's lucky."

"Maybe not. Look."

Another half dozen cruisers came into view just around the next bend in the road, strung along a grassy area next to the shoulder. Three of them were parked behind vehicles that had been pulled over, a different state trooper standing next to each and writing a ticket. A fourth officer waved down the Corvette, signaling the driver to pull over.

"A friend of mine who has a place up in Vermont told me about this, Timmy. One cruiser waits by the side of the highway just past a bend in the road, of which there are plenty on the Taconic. The officer trains his radar on the spot where the cars will come into sight. When he spots a speeder, he radios ahead to his fellow troopers lying in wait around the next bend, and they take turns pulling people over and issuing tickets. Nice and efficient. I think I'll keep my cruise control set at fifty-eight."

"Good idea."

They drove on in silence for a while, until Timmy asked his father about the place where they were hoping to meet up with Mrs. Murphy's son the next day, the place called the Smokey House Center at Danby Four Corners.

"I don't know much about it," Tim said. "I'm told it's up in the mountains about fifty miles north of the Massachusetts border. They say it sits on five thousand acres of preserved forest and farmland, and that it serves as an educational center for young people, willing to learn about the environment and sound farming methods. I think that may also include troubled youths, but of that I'm not certain. Either way, it seems like a nice idea, but I'm not sure what the attraction is for Hanny. It may just be the opportunity to lead this hike. I don't know. I guess we'll find out tomorrow."

"Are we sleeping there tonight?"

"No, it's not a hotel. We'll be staying in a town called Manchester, twenty miles down the road from Smokey House. There's an old inn called the 1811 House. I thought it might be a fun place to stay, and they had a room for one night because of a cancellation. On a big weekend like this during peak leaf season, you usually have to book three nights, but we got lucky."

The rest of the drive was uneventful. After a while, Timmy lost interest in the passing scenery, and spent some time studying for a history test he had to take on Tuesday. At five o'clock they rolled into the Village of Manchester.

"Here we are."

Tim slowed as they approached a large colonial structure with white-painted wood siding, a row of columns along the front, and green shutters on the windows.

"Is that the hotel we're staying at?"

"Nope. That's the Equinox Hotel. A little history there, too. Abraham Lincoln was supposed to stay at the Equinox in the summer in 1865, but he fell victim to an assassin's bullet a few months before. Some years later, his son Robert Todd Lincoln purchased an estate nearby, and built a beautiful summer home for himself. It's called Hildene, and it's still there. Maybe you can throw some of that in for extra credit on your exam on Tuesday."

"Where's the inn we're staying at?"

"Right over here."

He pointed to a much smaller, light brown building resembling an old farmhouse as he made a right turn. A sign hanging from a post in front identified it as the 1811 House.

Tim pulled into a small parking lot next to the building. They got out of the car, walked to the front door and entered. Hearing the door open, a casually dressed gentleman looked around the corner from another room.

"Checking in, or just stopping by for a drink?"

"We're checking in. My name's O'Leary, and this is my son, Timmy."

"Oh, right. You're the guy who lucked out when we had the cancellation. Well, why don't we take care of checking in later? Come into the pub with me. I'm just setting up for happy hour."

He motioned them to follow him toward the back of the building, where they entered a cozy, paneled room with a small bar.

"This is the pub. We open to guests and non-guests alike every evening for a couple of hours," the man said. "Have a seat and I'll get you something to drink."

He went around to the other side of the bar.

"Long ride?"

"About four hours," Tim said. "Nice ride. It's beautiful up here."

"That it is. The wife and I moved up to Manchester and bought this place two years ago. Before that, we lived in New Jersey for fifty years. What'll you have?"

Remembering his stay at Jay Peak, Tim ordered a bottle of Sam Adams.

"You got it. Hey, guess what? I hear Andy Pherson's getting ready to put out a Vermont ale real soon. Some say he's going to call it Long Trail Ale after the hiking trail that runs north-south up the spine of the Green Mountains. Maybe next time you're up, hey?"

"I'll look forward to trying it."

"And how about you, young man?" the innkeeper said. "Why don't you give our apple cider a try? It's made right here in East Dorset, at Mad Tom Orchard. Good place to go apple picking. You're a little late for that, though. Season just ended."

"Thanks," Timmy said. "Is that what they call hard cider, Mr. ... ?"

"Call me Billy, son, but no, I'm afraid this ain't that kind of cider. You'll like it, though."

He busied himself for a few minutes getting their drinks, as Tim and Timmy looked around.

"Why don't you two sit out on the back patio," he said. "I'll bring your drinks out there. It's not too chilly this evening, and the view of the mountains is great."

They went outside, where the view was indeed breathtaking.

"This is really nice," Timmy said. "I can see why Mrs. O'Leary's son likes it so much up here. Do you think he'll just stay?"

"He might, Timmy, but for now he's got some business he's going to have to attend to in New York. I hope he agrees to come back."

— 44 —

THE NEXT MORNING dawned clear and chilly. A dusting of frost covered the mountain peaks to their right and left as they drove north, while the lower slopes were still clad in brilliant autumn foliage. On either side of the road were pastures dotted with grazing cows and fields covered with stumps of corn stalks left behind from the late summer harvest.

"How far away is the place we're going to, dad?"

"The map says about a dozen miles to Danby, then about 4 miles up into the mountains until we get to Danby Four Corners. Once we get there, we'll check in at the office of the Smokey House Center, and see if they've had any word from Hanny yet. I doubt it, though. I called this morning, and the lady there said they don't expect the hikers back until lunchtime. She said they usually have some breakfast out on the trail the last morning, before dropping their tents and hiking the last few miles back to the Center."

"So, what do we do in the meantime?"

"I think it would be fun to walk around the Center and see what they do up there. She said they'd be happy to have one of the boys show us around."

"Look. That sign says Mad Tom Orchard. Isn't that the place Billy told us about yesterday? Where you can pick apples?"

"It must be. And I think he said Emerald Lake was just a little bit further up. This might be a great place for us to visit next summer."

Driving on, they passed the lake and a small shop selling folk art. Then the road opened up again, and they drove north in a wide valley, with mountains flanking it on either side. Billy had told them out on the patio the night before that the valley was bounded by the Taconic Mountains to the west and the Green Mountains to the east, and that they would find Danby about five miles further up the road.

Several minutes later, they saw a sign indicating that Danby was to their left. Turning, Tim wondered why the town was situated over a block west of the main road, and then realized that the town was probably there long before this road was built. Everything here seemed to go "way back." Concentrating harder now, he began the long, twisting climb up the mountain toward Danby Four Corners. About ten minutes later, they pulled into what appeared to be a large farm.

"This is it? I thought there was supposed to be a town called Danby Four Corners."

"Maybe that was the intersection we just turned off. It had four corners, right?"

"But that doesn't make it a town, does it?"

"You got me, Timmy, but I guess things are different up here. Anyway, here we are."

The two of them got out of the car and walked toward the big building that Tim assumed must house the Center's office. They entered the building, saw a door to the left, and looked inside. A middle-aged lady sitting at a desk saw them and smiled.

"Can I help you?"

"Yes, if you would. My son and I are here to see Hannibal Murphy. He's due in this morning with his camping group. My name is Tim O'Leary, and this is my son Timmy."

Realizing he had just said 'Hannibal,' Tim braced himself for the usual amused response.

Surprisingly, none came. Instead, the lady's smile widened. "Oh, what a nice young man. Welcome to the Smokey House Center, you two. I think Hanny, if I might call him that, as much as I just adore his full name, should be back shortly. You must be the gentleman who called this morning."

"Yes, that was me. Do you think we could look around while we wait?"

"I can do even better than that. I'll have Marjorie show you around. Why don't you sit down while I call over to the dormitory?"

She picked up the phone on her desk.

A few minutes later, a cute teenaged girl with ponytails, a plaid shirt and overalls poked her head through the door.

"Are you the guys who're here for the tour?" she said.

Timmy jumped to his feet. This was better than a boy. "Yes, that's us. Me and my dad. We're ready."

Tim rose more slowly, realizing for the first time that his son really was a teenager now. He thanked the lady behind the desk and followed Timmy and their guide out the door.

Over the next forty-five minutes, they saw pigs, cows, chickens, hay, tractors, and everything else that made the place a genuine farming operation, including a full complement of teenagers and pre-teens working diligently to keep the place running, and seeming to be doing so with only minimal adult supervision and guidance.

The girl walking Tim and Timmy around informed them that the center's primary function was to sustain traditional farming methods and the conservation of woodlands, by educating young people from the area about the preservation of their rural heritage. She said the Center had five thousand acres of forest and farmland which it intended to protect for future generations.

Tim was impressed. Timmy was smitten.

"Maybe I could spend some time here when we come up next summer, dad," Timmy said. "You did say we were coming, didn't you?"

"Well, sure ... maybe, that is. I mean ... wait a minute. I think that's Hanny."

Hanny came walking down the driveway with a dozen or so of his charges, who were lugging camping gear and looking like they were ready for a decent meal and a good night's sleep.

Tim waved.

"Over here, Hanny. Over here."

Hanny turned and spoke to his group, who nodded and walked toward the big house. He came over to where Tim, Timmy and their guide were standing.

"Hey, Tim! What are you doing up here?"

"There have been some developments in your father's estate. I think you're going to have to come back to New York with us today. There's something we need to take care of. It's urgent."

Their guide, sensing this was something personal, excused herself.

"Is it my mother?" Hanny said. "Is she okay? And who is this?"

"Your mother is fine, and this is my son, Timmy. He and I drove up to Manchester yesterday. I thought he'd enjoy seeing a little of Vermont. Today is Columbus Day, so he had no school."

"Hi, Timmy. Nice to meet you. Your dad's a good lawyer, so I guess he must think whatever is going on is important, but I'm supposed to lead another group out tomorrow."

He looked at Tim.

"Can we put this off for a week or two, Tim? It's probably my last trek of the season. I'll be free after that."

"Hanny, I'd love to say yes, but I don't think that's such a good idea. Why don't we go into town and have lunch? We can talk about it there."

Hanny laughed.

"There aren't any restaurants in this 'town,' Tim. We're just an intersection. Come on inside. We'll have lunch right here."

The three of them went back into the big farm building, where Hanny led them to a cafeteria-style dining area. He was greeted by his hiking group, seated at two of what looked like picnic tables scattered around the room.

"Hey, it's our fearless leader! Did you park the elephants out by the cow pasture?"

Tim rolled his eyes. Here we go again.

Hanny, unfazed, laughed.

"Nah, they were having too much fun stomping on the knapsacks you left out by the door."

Gesturing to Tim and Timmy, he led them to the cafeteria line on the other side of the room.

"Get what you want, guys. I'm right behind you. Then we can sit down so your dad can tell me what's on his mind, Timmy. Food's pretty good, and good for you. It's all farm raised."

The three of them helped themselves to some fresh vegetables and meat. Tim and Timmy then followed Hanny to a table on the far side of the room.

"So, what's going on with my father's estate, Tim?"

"Your uncle Chris moved away suddenly. He didn't even tell his secretary he was leaving. As you know, he didn't show up in court on the day he was ordered to, and it looks like he tried to take your father's estate assets with him when he left town. We got lucky there, at least. The account is at EF Hutton, and they refused to let him transfer it to Arizona, which is where we think he's gone. The court has now revoked his appointment as executor, and the estate account is frozen for the time being."

"You did all that? I told you your dad is a good lawyer, didn't I, Timmy?"

He looked back at Tim. "So why do I have to rush back

to New York? It sounds like you've got everything under control. Can't it wait for a couple of weeks?"

"No, Hanny, it can't. The estate is invested in all kinds of speculative investments, and only an executor can get rid of them. We need to get one appointed right away."

"All right, I'll see if I can get someone to cover for me tomorrow."

They finished lunch, and Hanny excused himself while he stepped into the office to see what could be done about his schedule. Returning a few minutes later, he gave them the thumbs up.

"Okay, Tim. Maisie is going to ask her older brother to take my group tomorrow, and then I'll take his on Friday."

"Maisie?"

"She's the girl who showed us around today," Timmy said.

"I thought her name was Marjorie?" his father asked.

"She told me I should call her Maisie. She also gave me her phone number, in case I had any questions later."

Tim looked at Hanny, who smiled.

"Cute, isn't she, Timmy?"

Timmy blushed.

"It was just if I had any questions."

"Right. Anyway, let me pack a few things, and then we can go."

"Well, okay, then," Tim said, still absorbing Timmy's transition.

An hour later, they were on the road. The drive back to New York was uneventful, although traffic began to slow as more and more cars joined the Columbus Day weekenders returning to the city.

The sun was just setting to the west as they pulled up in front of Mrs. Murphy's apartment in Co-op City. Hanny retrieved his bag and said good night, promising to meet Tim at the office in the morning. Then he thought of something. He stopped and looked back.

"So, who's going to be the executor?"

"You are, Hanny."

"Me? I don't know how to be an executor."

"You're going to have to learn fast. We have a lot to do in the next couple of days."

The understatement of the year.

— 45 —

MRS. MURPHY ARRIVED at the office bright and early on Tuesday morning, with a spruced up Hanny in tow. He was
clean-shaven and wore a button-down shirt, dress slacks,
and new shoes.

"Here's your new executor, Mr. O'Leary. I made him
dress appropriately."

Hanny smiled.

"My mother made me go out last night and buy a new
shirt, a pair of dress slacks, and new shoes. She even made
me shave. There was no talking her out of it, but I think I
look ridiculous. What's next? Some kind of coronation cer-
emony?"

Tim laughed.

"Nothing that formal, Hanny, but I'm glad you dressed
up a bit. You and I are going down to the courthouse today.
Mrs. Murphy, I need you to type up a few things first."

"Certainly, Mr. O'Leary. Just let me take off my coat, and
we can get right to work." She was smiling broadly as she
hurried off to the closet.

"Hanny, let's talk a bit while your mother is getting set

up. Why don't you come into my office and sit down?"

Hanny complied, and for the next hour, he and Tim went over the plan for the day. Essentially, it would involve signing some documents and taking them to the Bronx County Courthouse, where the Surrogate's Court had its offices. Tim had prepared drafts of the documents at home the night before, and he had left them on Mrs. Murphy's desk this morning. Once she typed them, there would probably be the need to make a few revisions, and then the final versions could be signed and notarized. After that, he and Hanny would take them to the courthouse, and deliver them to the court's law department.

Tim had called Connie Logan earlier. She was already at her desk at eight in the morning. They discussed the situation, and arrived at an acceptable procedure for getting Hanny appointed.

Normally, a formal application would have had to be made, on notice to all affected persons, giving them a reasonable opportunity to be heard on the application. This would have been done by the filing of a written petition, advising the court of the specifics of the application. The court would then issue a formal notice, called a citation, letting those persons know what was going on. The citation would give them a specific date and time when they could come to the court and present their points of view. Only then could the judge make a decision.

Even if no one objected, the whole process would typically take weeks, if not longer.

In this case, however, time was of the essence, given what had happened with the estate account. Over the phone the week before, Connie Logan and Tim had mutually devised a streamlined procedure, based on three key facts. First, there was no executor in place, Chris Murphy having been summarily removed. Second, since Hanny wouldn't turn twenty-five for several more weeks, the entire estate was distributable to the trust created for him by his father, with Madeline

Murphy as trustee. Third, although the Will named no sub-
stitute executor, there was a qualified person willing to take
on the responsibilities of administering the estate as an administrator c.t.a., that job being essentially the same as that
of an executor. The qualified person, of course, was Hannibal Murphy.

Based on these factors, Tim told Hanny, the court was
willing to expedite matters in a fairly straightforward manner. Hanny would sign a petition seeking appointment as the
administrator c.t.a. of his father's estate. Mrs. Murphy, as
trustee, would consent in writing to that appointment, and
waive the usual formal notice of the application. These documents, once notarized in the appropriate manner, would be
filed with the court along with a proposed order, and the order would be submitted to the judge. Barring any problems,
the judge would sign the order, which would appoint Hanny
to take over the administration of his father's estate.

Tim stopped, and took a breath.

"Got that, Hanny?"

"But, Tim, you still haven't told me what an executor, or
what did you call it, an administrator, actually does."

"Basically, he or she collects the deceased person's assets,
pays things like debts, funeral expenses, and taxes, and then
distributes what's left, after paying the expenses of getting all
this done, to the beneficiary. In this case, that would be you,
or the trust your father set up for you.

"How do I find out who my father owed money to, or
how much has to be paid in taxes, and all that other stuff?"

"You won't have to. As near as we can tell, all that's been
taken care of already. The problem is, your uncle never got
around to the part about turning over what was left to your
trust. Instead, he hung on to the estate, took fees, commissions, and expenses he had no right to take without court approval, and invested the funds in what looks like an attempt
to make a killing on the market, presumably anticipating he
could live off the estate forever."

"What kind of companies did he invest in?"

"Big ones, I guess. It's all in the papers over at the court-house."

"How have they been doing?"

"Believe it or not, they've been doing well. Very well, actually. The estate has doubled in value over the last year. It's now worth about four million dollars, but things have started to slow down lately. That hasn't stopped him from being aggressive, though. I guess he figured all those puts and calls, and investing on margin, would work forever."

"Tim, I don't know anything about investing. Maybe I should just leave everything the way it is. I mean, after all, that's a tremendous amount of money. I don't have to try to make it even bigger. So what if the market stops going up, or even if it goes back down a little. Four million is fine—Better than fine."

"Hanny, listen. I don't know a lot about investing, either, but I do know it could get a lot worse than that. Take margin, for example. Suppose you'd like to buy a stock that costs $200, but you only have $100, so you can't. Except that your broker says oh, yes, you can. We'll just lend you a hundred dollars. That's called a margin loan. So, you buy the stock, and then it goes up to $300. You sell it, pay back the hundred you borrowed, and you now have $200. You just doubled your money."

"What's wrong with that?"

"What's wrong is what happens if the stock doesn't go up. What if it goes down, down from $200 to $100? You still owe $100, so you'll have to sell the stock, which is now worth only $100, and pay off the hundred-dollar margin loan. What are you left with then?"

"Nothing, I guess."

"Right. You are left with nothing, even though the stock lost only half its value, not all of it. In other words, investing on margin is like gambling. You can hit the jackpot, but you can also go bust."

"I see, and what were those other things you mentioned? Puts and calls."

"Again, they have to do with leveraging your investments, so you can make more with less, but why don't I leave that to Mr. Baker over at EF Hutton to explain? We're going to meet with him after we get you appointed administrator. Stay put for a minute. I want to see how your mother is doing with those papers."

Tim stepped outside his office just in time to see Mrs. Murphy rising from her chair with a fistful of typed sheets in her hand.

"All done, Mr. O'Leary."

She handed them to Tim, who riffled through and looked up.

"Good job, as always, Mrs. Murphy. Give me a few minutes to go through these, and then we can put them in final."

"Yes sir, Mr. O'Leary. We have a special client to take care of here." She smiled and sat back down.

The papers required little revision, and within a half hour, the signing and notarizing had been done. Tim stuffed everything into his briefcase, and he and Hanny left the office. A taxi Mrs. Murphy had called for them idled by the curb.

Connie Logan was waiting at the courthouse, Tim having called ahead. She told him the judge was standing by to sign the order appointing the son as administrator c.t.a. if everything was in order.

Which it was.

After waiting briefly for the clerk to issue a certificate evidencing Hanny's appointment, Tim and Hanny left the courthouse and took another cab to the EF Hutton office. They found Mr. Baker sitting behind his desk, reading a copy of the Wall Street Journal. He looked up, and, recognizing Tim, greeted them with a smile.

"Good morning. I didn't expect to see you this soon. The account's still here, in case you were wondering. And who is this young man? Wait ... let me guess. Could it be the mighty

Hannibal himself? Hah!"

"Did my uncle tell you about me?"

Baker squinted and then raised his eyebrows.

"No, you're pulling my leg, right? Your name isn't really Hannibal, is it?"

Now Hanny was confused. He looked at Tim.

"Sorry, Hanny, I forgot to tell you. Mr. Baker thought I was joking when I told him your name. Mr. Baker, I'd like you to meet Hannibal Murphy, the son of the late Francis Murphy and the nephew of your former customer, Chris Murphy. Hanny, this is Halbert Baker. He's the broker for the estate's investment account."

Baker stood up and shook Hanny's hand.

"Do I call you Hannibal, or do you prefer Mr. Murphy?"

"Hanny works for me, Mr. Baker."

"As does Hal for me. So, now that we've got the introductions out of the way, why don't you two sit down?"

Baker pointed to the two chairs across from him. Once they were settled, he asked Tim where things stood with the appointment of a new executor.

"Believe it or not, Hal, we have one already. Hanny has been appointed administrator c.t.a. of his father's estate. The judge signed off on it this morning, and here's a certificate evidencing his appointment for your operations department."

He slid it across the desk.

"That was fast. Congratulations, young man. I'll get this certificate over to our operations department so they can change the name on the account. I'm sure they'll have some paperwork for you to complete also, but in the meantime let's talk about what you'd like to do with the investments."

"I really don't know, Mr. Baker."

"Hal."

"Right, Hal. Sorry. I just don't know a thing about investing."

Tim tried to help.

"I've talked to Hanny about some of the riskier aspects

of his uncle's investment strategies, but I think it would be better if you could spend some time going over the account with him, and giving him the benefit of your expertise. Then he'd be better able to make some decisions."

"Sure, Mr. O'Leary."

"Tim."

"Okay, Tim. How about this?" Baker said. "It's almost lunchtime. I'll call in an order to one of the local restaurants that delivers. The three of us can sit in our conference room, and I can show Hanny the estate account's holdings, and give him the opportunity to review any printed research we have that's relevant to the securities in the account."

"That sounds great, Hal, but I'm going to have to excuse myself. I need to get back to the office so I can catch up on a couple of things. Okay with you, Hanny?"

"Sure, Tim. I'll call if I need to speak to you."

"Good. When are you heading back to Vermont?"

"Thursday morning. I'm taking the bus. I need to be back for Friday's hike."

"Okay. Have a safe trip. We can talk again when you return."

46

"SO, WHAT DO YOU THINK I should do, Hal?"

Hal was concentrating on his cheeseburger. He looked up.

"Hard to say, Hanny. There's a lot of money here, but some of your uncle's bets are pretty risky. Maybe we should talk about what you want to do with your life. Your uncle said you disappeared and were never heard from again, and that that's why he couldn't wrap up the estate. Why would he say something like that? I mean, you're right here sitting in front of me."

Hanny shrugged. "Well, he was sort of right, at least in a way. I did travel around Central and South America for several years, studying the remains of ancient civilizations. I didn't keep in touch, I'll admit, but from what I've been told, he should have turned over the money to my mother once all the debts and taxes were paid. She was supposed to invest it as my trustee. Anyway, I've been back in the states for a couple of months now, and Tim started pressing my uncle to do what he was supposed to do. I guess that's why he ran, and tried to take it with him."

"Quite a story, Hanny. Sounds like you got lucky. What

are your plans, now that you're back?"

"I think I'd like to do something up in Vermont. Before I wandered into the state when I finally found my way back, I was trying to understand why the great structures of the earth were erected at such cost."

"You mean how much money was spent?"

"No, I mean human cost."

"How so?"

"Slave labor, physical suffering, wars. Most of the structures were monuments to human vanity, as far as I could tell. From what I learned during my travels, the costs didn't necessarily stop when the construction was complete. Some of those 'temples' were regularly used for human sacrifice, others as the backdrop for more wars and oppression. And in the end, they all wound up in ruins."

"So, you gave up?"

"You might say that, but then I stumbled onto Vermont. When I got there and looked around, I realized we don't have to build anything. It's already been built for us. The sky, the mountains, the lakes, the rivers, everything. It's all there for us to enjoy and protect."

"That sounds nice, Hanny, but how are we supposed to protect it?"

"By respecting it. No wars, no temples. Build what we need to live, not what we think will glorify ourselves. Use what it gives us, but preserve its ability to continue to do so."

"I like what I'm hearing, Hanny, but what does that have to do with your father's estate?"

"I'd like to use it to help what they're doing up there in Vermont. How do you invest for that?"

Hal chuckled.

"I'm afraid EF Hutton doesn't have much of a track record there, Hanny. I guess word about what's been going on around here didn't make its way down to you in South America."

"What do you mean?"

"Check kiting, wire fraud, you name it. Copped a plea on that one. Now last week, word comes out that the feds are planning to indict the firm for laundering money for some crime bosses up in Rhode Island. Some of the guys are talking about getting out of here, going to some other brokerage firm. I'm one of them. Who wants to be part of an operation like this?"

"That sounds awful, Hal. Was the company always like this?"

"Just the opposite. We've been around for over eighty years. It was the kind of place a lot of us admired when we first got into the business. It's a shame, but I guess some of what you were describing filtered its way in. People saw a way to build monuments to themselves—mansions, yachts, buildings named after themselves, dinners in their honor, the more the better. If the customers of some little bank in the boondocks, or some victims of the crime bosses, got hurt in the process, no big deal. If the people pulling these stunts even thought about it, they probably figured that's simply the way the world works."

"Even if they didn't feel guilty, once they had made what they needed, why didn't they stop?"

"They couldn't. I think they figured why should they stop? They probably forgot what they were shooting for in the beginning. Either that or they thought they could always use some more, so why not?"

"But in the end, they got caught. Kind of like the temple builders, except some of them didn't exactly get caught. They died."

"That catches up with all of us eventually, so maybe we should get back to what we're supposed to be talking about. What shall we do with your father's estate account?"

They continued to discuss investment options until the market closed at four. By then, it was apparent that nothing would be accomplished by going over the options indefinitely. Decisions had to be made.

"Or you could do nothing, and let it ride," was Hal's final suggestion, as he rose and started to leave the room.

"You can use the conference room until closing time if you'd like, so you can go over these papers again," he said, walking toward the door. "The market's closed now, so maybe you should just sleep on it. Why don't you give me a call in the morning and tell me what you want to do. I get in early."

But Hanny didn't call.

47

"I CAN'T BELIEVE how accommodating they were at Bronx Surrogate's. That's never happened for me before, not ever, and I've been in practice for almost twenty years."

"What happened, exactly?" Marge said.

"An attorney in the law department named Connie Logan saw the problem right away. She was creative and fast. She had no sympathy for Chris Murphy types, and she made sure we had what we needed to get the situation under control before anyone got hurt. As of this afternoon, Hanny Murphy has the reins, and when I left them, Hal Baker was giving him a crash course on investing. Another couple of weeks and the estate should be cleaned up, and Hanny's inheritance will be his father's present to him on his twenty-fifth birthday."

"Geez, I forgot all about that. Twenty-five is a real milestone. Maybe we should have Hanny and his mother over on his birthday to celebrate."

"Or maybe he's the one who should be throwing the party, with all the money he'll be coming into."

"But didn't you say the estate was in very risky investments? Couldn't he lose a lot?"

"Maybe a little, I guess, while he and Hal sort through things and make some decisions, but we're talking about four million dollars. There's plenty of time to review the situation and start unwinding the risky stuff–the puts and calls, the margin loans. Worst case, let's say the account drops a couple hundred thousand in the meantime. I'm not saying it will, but even that's only five percent. Who knows? Maybe they'll actually make a few dollars. The important thing is that we got there in time, before Chris Murphy made off with the whole estate."

"I suppose, but I think we'll all breathe a little easier when this is over."

"Amen to that. So, what's on the agenda for the rest of the week?"

"Timmy has soccer practice tomorrow, and Katie has her first rehearsal for the school play in December. She finally figured out that a 'smitch' isn't a 'snitch,' but she still wants to know what it means. We're working on that."

"Glad you're making progress."

"Oh, and I have a new client. Her name is Mary. I can't tell you her last name, of course, since it's confidential. She says she was adopted at birth, but has a pretty good idea who her natural mother is."

"Who is it?"

"She thinks it was a teenage neighbor of her adoptive parents. A girl who, as they say, 'got in trouble.' Mary has no regrets about having been given up for adoption. She was raised in a loving environment by her adoptive parents, and she's happy for that. Recently, though, she learned of a new development that could prove to be a financial boon, if she's right about who her birth mother was."

"What kind of development?"

"Over the years, Mary's adoptive parents often talked about a girl from the neighborhood who had lived a sad life. That poor girl's name was Sandra. Sandra's parents had died in an accident when she was still quite young. She had struggled to cope, but she was fortunate in one respect. Several years after her parents passed away, Sandra's grandfather had set up a trust for her, and from then on, at least, she had financial security. She couldn't touch the principal of the trust, but the income would be hers for life. After her death, the trust would pay out to her children, if there were any. Otherwise it would go to a charity."

"Is Sandra still alive?"

"Yes, although a few years ago, Sandra became quite ill. She was treated, and experienced some temporary relief, but the prognosis was poor. The illness would come back, and would eventually take her life. She decided not to wait for that to happen. She told some friends she was going to travel and see the world, while she was still able to do so."

"How does this relate to Mary?"

"Mary's adoptive parents are both deceased. They died from natural causes. First her mother, and a few years later, her father. Just before he passed, he told her what she had always suspected—that Sandra was her birth mother. Nothing was written down, but Mary still thinks she might be able to prove it. Her belief is based on not only what her adoptive father told her, but on a number of things people have said over the years. It would still be better, of course, if Sandra herself was willing to confirm it. If Mary is Sandra's daughter, the trust should come to her when Sandra dies, she being Sandra's only child. She'd also like to meet the person who brought her into this world."

"But you said Mary was adopted," Tim said. "That would cut off her right to take the trust remainder as a child of her birth mother."

"Yes, but there's a twist. It turns out that Mary was never formally adopted. She had thought she was, but when her father told her about Sandra being her mother, he also confessed that there hadn't been a formal adoption."

"Why not?"

"He said they had acted as foster parents at first, wanting

to see if it would work out, and also thinking Sandra might change her mind and decide she wanted to raise her child herself. Time passed, the arrangement never really changed, and the so-called adoptive parents gradually forgot about a formal adoption, thinking it might be better not to give the birth mother any second thoughts."

"Where is Sandra now?"

"That's just it," Marge said. "No one knows. With my help, Mary hopes to find her."

"How would you do that?" Tim said.

"We need more information about the grandfather's trust, so I'll have to track down the lawyers who put it together. I need to know who and where the trustee is, and see where the income checks have been going since Sandra started her travels. Even if the payments were being direct deposited into her bank account, instead of being made with checks, I'd like to know the location of the bank. If I knew that, it would at least be a starting point in trying to find her."

"What if you do find out who the lawyers are and what bank is involved? You don't think they'll give you any information, do you? It's probably attorney-client privileged, or in the case of the bank, confidential."

"To some extent, yes, but if I can convince the lawyers that my client is possibly a beneficiary of the trust, they should at least advise the trustee that she's entitled to be informed about the trust and its assets so she can have the opportunity to establish her claim."

Laughing, she added, "If they stonewall me, I might need your services, Mr. Attorney."

"My fees are too high for you."

"Maybe you could take it out in trade," she said with a smile, putting her arms around him.

"Hmm, sounds like a plan. I'll have Mrs. Murphy type up a retainer letter in the morning."

48

TIM CALLED HAL BAKER on Wednesday afternoon to see what he and Hanny had decided to do with the estate account. Hal told him about their lengthy meeting on Tuesday afternoon, and said that Hanny, although a quick study, needed time to absorb what he had learned before making any major decisions. Hal had suggested that Hanny give him a call this morning with any additional questions he might have, but he hadn't heard from him yet. In the meantime, the operations department had reviewed the certificate Tim had brought with him the day before, and had authorized Hal to act upon Hanny's instructions regarding the estate account.

"How's the market holding up, Hal?"

"To tell you the truth, Tim, it's a little rocky. For God's sake, by late August, the Dow was up forty-four percent for the year. You could say it was high time for it to take a breather. In fact, it gave back a chunk of the forty-four over the next month, but Chris Murphy never flinched. He doubled down on his bets. Then the market started climbing again, and by the time we got into October, it had taken back half of what it had lost. Chris was probably ecstatic, but I'll never know. That was about the time he went AWOL."

"So, we're holding our own?"

"Not really. We've already given back that little bump, and a chunk more. This week we've been just holding our breath. We're down almost a hundred points today, or close to four percent, and who knows what tomorrow may bring."

"Okay, Hal. Let's hope things settle down. I appreciate your help. I guess you know Hanny is going back up to Vermont tomorrow. He's leading a group on an eight-day hike in the Taconic Mountains, starting some time on Friday. He's probably a little preoccupied with that, but I'm sure he'll be in touch when he gets back. Then the two of you can begin the process of unwinding some of what you correctly referred to as Chris Murphy's 'bets.'"

"Will do, Tim. I'll be on vacation for a week starting next Tuesday, or maybe Monday if I can swing it. I'll be back in the office the week after next, so I'll be here when he returns."

Tim hung up, and tried to concentrate on the other matters that had piled up on his desk while the business of the Murphy estate consumed him.

— 49 —

ON THURSDAY MORNING, Hanny boarded a bus at the Port Authority Bus Terminal in Manhattan that would take him as far as Albany. Once there, he was to transfer to a Vermont Trailways bus, which would bring him into Vermont at Bennington, and then turn north toward Danby.

His window seat afforded dramatic views of the fall scenery, but he couldn't concentrate on the passing panorama, or the hike he would be leading out of the Smokey House Center in the morning. Instead, he kept thinking about his father's estate account and what he had finally decided to do about it during a mostly sleepless night.

Hal Baker had been very helpful in explaining the options available to him, and sympathetic with respect to Hanny's insecurity in dealing with sums this large. Nevertheless, he had repeatedly declined Hanny's entreaties that Hal make the decisions that needed to be made. Those were Hanny's responsibility now, he said.

Three hours after leaving the Port Authority, the bus pulled into a parking area in Albany, and Hanny got off. He walked across the pavement and entered the terminal for Vermont Trailways.

Taking a seat inside, he still felt uneasy about his decision. He knew he should communicate it to Hal Baker before he set out on the eight-day hike scheduled to begin tomorrow morning, but he was frightened that he might be making a terrible mistake. What if he was wrong? Maybe he should wait until he came back, when he could give it more thought.

Ten minutes later, the desk clerk announced the arrival of the bus that would drop him off in Danby on its way further north. He stood up and headed to the door, went outside and saw it. Half in a daze, he walked across the lot and climbed the steps into the bus. Still distracted, he started toward the seats, when the driver spoke up.

"Your ticket, sir?"

"Oh, sorry."

Hanny fished the ticket out of his pocket and handed it to the driver. "Thank you, sir," the man said. "Danby, is it?"

"That's right. Somebody from Smokey House Center is going to give me a ride from there up to Danby Four Corners."

"Well, Danby is a flag stop. Not too much call for picking up passengers there, and even less for dropping them off. Make sure you remind me when we get close, or I might drive right past it."

"Okay, thanks. I'll be sure to do that."

He stepped away and looked down the aisle. There were plenty of available seats, but, heedful of the driver's request to be reminded of his destination when they were close to Danby, Hanny chose the seat right behind him. Other passengers filtered in, but not too many, and the bus was less than half full when it pulled away from the terminal fifteen minutes later.

He closed his eyes and tried to sleep, but without much success. Who was he to think he could make a decision about matters like this? He knew nothing about finance, much less the exotic concepts he used to talk about. He must have been kidding himself when he pretended to be on a quest to find the meaning of life—the "theory of everything."

The day was still sunny. As they drove east from Albany, the hills grew taller, until mountains replaced them as the bus entered Vermont. Hanny finally drifted off to sleep.

"There's the Old First Church."

He opened his eyes with a start.

"What?"

"Oh, sorry, kid. I didn't realize you were asleep."

It was the bus driver. He was looking at Hanny in his rear-view mirror.

Looking back at the road, he continued.

"I have a habit of telling people about things like that, especially around this time of the year, when we have so many tourists riding with us. It's sort of like a free tour for the leaf peepers. Some appreciate it so much they give me a tip when they get off the bus."

"That's all right, Mr. ... "

"Jones. Bobby Jones, like the golfer. No relation, of course. You up here to sightsee, or something else?"

"Something else, I guess, Mr. Jones. I have a part-time job leading hikers on camping trips in the mountains. I have one going out tomorrow from the Smokey House Center."

"Do you? That's an interesting place. Some of the kids from my town sign up for the programs up there in the summertime. Some of them need a little help in getting along in this new world we live in. Better to learn about taking care of animals than betting on them at the track."

"You have race tracks up here?"

"Sure. Right down in Pownal, just south of here."

"I didn't know about that. Are the horse races still going on, or is the season over?"

"Horse races? No, dogs. They race greyhounds down there. You want horse races, you'll have to go over to Saratoga. They're closed for the season now, though. Whoops, I'd better concentrate. My first stop is right up ahead."

Tim stared out the window and his thoughts quickly returned to his father's estate. He'd have to call Hal Baker as soon as he got off the bus in Danby. Or should he wait?

As they progressed up Route 7 after a brief stop in Bennington, Tim noticed a forested hillside with an unusual feature. There was one tree in the midst of a multitude of others that was significantly taller than the rest, probably by a good twenty feet.

"Mr. Jones?"

"Bobby, buddy. Call me Bobby. What's up?"

"There's a tree over there on the slope that's a lot taller than all the others. What type of tree is it?"

"Same as the rest. They're all spruce trees. That one just decided to grow a little taller. I've noticed it before. If you hike in there, you won't be able to distinguish it from the rest of them. They're all the same on the bottom. I like to think it just worked a little harder to get that tall. Not so it could lord it over the others, mind you, but so it could see the stars at night. Too bad most people aren't like that. They just want to get up there so they can look down on everyone else, and they don't care who they push out of the way in the process. Ah well, there I go again. Bobby Jones the philosopher."

Then it all came together for Hanny.

Awhile later, the bus pulled into a parking area in a town called Manchester Center, and stopped. The driver announced to the passengers that they could get out and stretch their legs if they'd like. The bus wouldn't be continuing on for another fifteen minutes.

Hanny jumped out and ran for a pay phone.

50

THE WEEKEND WAS QUIET. Then it was Monday, and Tim, back at his desk, looked forward to a quiet week, the Murphy estate crisis finally behind him.

"Mr. O'Leary, your wife is on the phone."

"Thank you, Mrs. Murphy."

He picked up.

"Hey, Marge. What's up?"

"Tim, something's wrong. It's all over the news. The stock market is crashing. They're starting to call it Black Monday."

"What? Crashing? How much is it down?"

"Ten, no fifteen, wait ... twenty percent so far. It's on the radio. It's a panic. Poor Hanny. He could get wiped out. Does Mrs. Murphy know?"

"No. We don't have a radio in the office. I'd better call Hal Baker. Twenty percent? That's awful, but hey, even if it's down that much, twenty percent of the estate account is still only about eight hundred thousand. That leaves over three million if it stops there."

Tim suddenly realized it wasn't that simple. He stood up and nervously paced back and forth, as far as the phone cord allowed.

"Oh my God, the margin loans. They're probably call-ing them left and right. Plus, the call options Chris Murphy bought—they must be worthless now. No one wants those things if everything is falling off a cliff. This is a train wreck. Marge, I've got to call Baker. Maybe he'll take instructions from me since Hanny is unreachable right now. We could at least try to save something before it's too late."

He paused briefly to listen.

"Yes, I'll tell him to sell, sell everything, see if we can sal-vage anything. Gotta go. Bye."

He hung up the phone, then looked up. Mrs. Murphy was standing at the door to his office.

"What's going on, Mr. O'Leary? Is something wrong? Is it Hanny?"

"It's the stock market, Mrs. Murphy. There's panic down on Wall Street. Marge heard it on the radio. The bottom's dropping out. I've got to call Hal Baker. Right now."

"Hanny's money?"

"Yes."

He snatched Baker's card off his desk and started to dial the number. Mrs. Murphy staggered toward his desk.

"Hello, hello. Oh, damn, I'm getting a recording. Some-thing about all their lines being busy. How could that be?"

He hung up.

"Let me try again."

Same result.

Mrs. Murphy slumped forward and buried her face in her right hand as she reached for the edge of the desk with her left.

"No, no, how can this have happened? For once, every-thing seemed like it was going to be okay. Oh, oh. I think I'm going to faint. I'd better sit down."

Tim pulled his jacket from the back of one of the client chairs, as Mrs. Murphy collapsed into the other.

"I'm going over there. Keep trying to get Mr. Baker on

the phone. If you get him, tell him I'm on my way. Tell him not to go anywhere."

Throwing his jacket over his shoulders, Tim rushed to the door. Once out on the street, he walked quickly to where his car was parked, jumped in, and started it up. Seeing an opening in the traffic, he gunned the engine, pulled out onto the street, and sped to the EF Hutton office. When he got there, he ignored the No Parking sign in front of the building, stopped the car, and got out.

Inside was bedlam. Brokers were at their desks or standing next to them, yelling into their phones and frantically pushing buttons on their computers. Customers were shouting at them, trying to get their attention. Stock symbols flew across a digital ticker tape on the back wall of the room. All were in red, with arrows pointing toward the floor. Tim raced over to Hal Baker's desk, and found it empty. He looked around.

"Where is Mr. Baker?"

No one even looked at him. He raised his voice and tried again. One of the harried brokers heard him, cupped his hand over the receiver on his phone, and yelled back.

"He called in sick today."

51

BY THE END OF THE DAY, the market was in tatters. The Dow Jones average had plummeted nearly twenty-three percent by the close of trading, on top of a ten percent decline over the last few days of the week before. Some experts were predicting that the losses would eventually be recovered, at least in part, if the markets were to stabilize over the ensuing days and weeks. At the same time, they acknowledged that the brutal effects of margin calls and options losses would make even this type of modest improvement impossible for more aggressively invested portfolios .

The newspapers carried front page banner headlines. On Tuesday morning, the front page of the normally staid New York Times shrieked:

STOCKS PLUNGE 508 POINTS, A DROP OF 22.6%
604 MILLION VOLUME NEARLY DOUBLES RECORD

The "record," of course, had been set in 1929, setting off the Great Depression.

By the time Tim and Marge sat down to dinner on Tuesday evening, the whole world had heard, except perhaps for a small group of hikers walking through the Vermont woods.

"What will this do to Hanny when he finds out?" Marge said. "The poor kid. He probably thought everything would be good now. He'd be very well off. He could help his mother, and maybe find a satisfying career for himself. How will you tell him?"

Tim looked down at his plate.

"I just don't know, Marge. I just don't know."

"I can call Maisie," Timmy said.

"Maisie?"

"You remember. She showed us around Smokey House Center when we were up there. I have her phone number."

"What would that do? Hanny is out on the trail and won't be back until Saturday."

"Maybe he'll get back early. I could tell her what's happening, and that I'll call every day to see if Hanny's back."

Tim resisted the temptation to roll his eyes. The priorities of a teenager in love. He looked away.

The full weight of the situation finally struck him. He couldn't let young Hanny find this out from a chance remark, overheard at the Stoney House Center on his return. Even worse might be a headline on a crumpled-up newspaper, lying in a wastebasket in the Center's cafeteria. One way or the other, the news was something that should be delivered in person. It was too heartbreaking to be conveyed second hand.

He put down his fork.

"You know what? I think I'd better tell him myself. I'm going to drive up there early Saturday and talk to him. When I went over to see Hal Baker yesterday, they told me Hal had called in sick. He's supposed to be on vacation starting today, so I suspect he figured he'd get an early start. Either way, I won't be able to talk to him until next week. Given that, I won't have much in the way of specifics for Hanny, but I still think he deserves to be told about the crash in person."

"I'll come with you, Dad," Timmy said.

"Timmy, you have two midterms on Monday," Marge interjected. "You're staying right here."

"Oh, mom, come on. I can study in the car."

"Sorry, babe. Maisie will just have to wait 'til next time. Tim, have you talked to Hanny's mother about this? Do you think you should ask her to drive up there with you?"

"I don't think so. She was devastated when she heard about what had happened. Seeing the two of us there when he gets back, and his mother probably an emotional wreck, would hit too hard and too fast. I'll try to break the news to Hanny as gently as I can, although he'll still know there must be something very wrong when he sees me waiting for him."

"You're going to wait outside for him to arrive?"

"I think so."

"I guess that makes sense. There's no point in trying to let him unwind first. It's unrealistic to think he'll be able to relax with his hikers, while they celebrate their safe return, and so on. I'm sure word of what's been going on will have reached even that outpost of civilization by then. Someone is bound to say something about it as soon as he walks in the door."

"Yes, someone likely will. Word of the crash will have found its way to Smokey House Center. It's headline news all over the country. Late editions of yesterday's papers were already screaming 'Panic! Bedlam! Jump! The End is Here!' And it's all over the news channels everywhere. No, he won't have walked out of the forest ten minutes before he hears what's happened."

"How do you think he'll take it?"

"Not good, I imagine. How else?"

"They ought to lock up that Chris Murphy. What a low-down creep he is. Do you think the police will find him?"

"I doubt they'll even look, Marge. It's not the kind of matter police departments have much time for. If he had managed to make off with the estate account, it might be a different story. But taking fees and commissions he had no right to? Making wildly speculative investments with an estate account? The cops would rather leave that kind of stuff to the lawyers and the civil courts. Anyway, I think I'll wake up early on Saturday and hit the road. Maybe I can get there before Hanny comes in."

*   *   *

As predicted, the markets stabilized somewhat over the next few days. By Saturday morning, the topics on the morning radio news reports had returned to more commonplace subjects. The St. Louis Cardinals had lost the first two games of the World Series to the Minnesota Twins, but had then returned home and won the next three. The Twins were going back to Minnesota behind three games to two, and hoping to stave off elimination in today's game six. Talk of Black Monday was quickly being relegated to footnote status.

Except, of course, for those who had gone down with the ship.

THE DAY BEFORE, on Friday afternoon, Hanny's hikers trudged along a path that meandered through the hills south of a town called Tinmouth. It was the last town they had passed through after leaving Smokey House Center a week earlier. Theirs was a novice group whose individuals had done only modestly arduous treks previously. It would be their last hike until the following spring, when they would move up to more difficult trails.

For the prior seven days, they had studied the flora and fauna, learned skills that would be required for subsisting in the woods, and cultivated methods to navigate to their planned destinations. They hiked west at first, through fields and forests, up moderate inclines and across shallow streams. Turning north, they progressed through a valley, with fields devoted to pasturing cows, breeding horses, and grazing sheep. They even cheated a little now and then, walking from time to time on paved roads. Eventually, after covering nearly thirty miles in five days, they reached the farthest point of their journey, arriving in a town called Poultney. They visited a small school there, aptly named Green Mountain College.

When one of the hikers realized where they were, he told Hanny his older brother was a student there, and offered to go find his brother and ask him if they could sleep in the dorm that night. Hanny, amused, declined, and led the group south and east until they reached a little town named Tinmouth a few days later. After a brief rest there, they walked south a short distance until they reached this evening's campsite.

The weather had been comfortable, with daily temperatures topping out in the mid-fifties, and even in the low sixties on occasion. Except for a few showers, there had been hardly any precipitation. The nights were chilly, in the twenties and thirties, but warm clothing, cozy tents and cushioned sleeping bags made sack time an agreeable end to the day.

Every evening, after pitching their tents and gathering dry wood from the surrounding forest, the boys would build a campfire and cook dinner. Because of restrictions on making fires in the Vermont back country, their campsites were always on private, undeveloped, lands, with the advance permission of the landowners, most of whom were strongly supportive of the Smokey House Center's mission. After eating, the group told stories around the campfire.

"So, Hanny, what was it like in the jungle?"

This from a thirteen-year-old named Ricky, who, like the others, had been permitted to skip school for a week, so he could learn about the environment. The local schools believed that this knowledge could best be obtained from close encounters with the unspoiled mountains of Vermont.

The question posed by Ricky was not original. It was essentially the same question one of the hikers would ask every night, tonight being Ricky's turn. Someone at Smokey House had told them about Hanny, after he had been assigned to lead them on this trip. The hikers were intrigued with Hanny's adventures in Central and South America

This would be the final night around the campfire for the group, and Hanny thought something special would be appropriate.

"Just a minute, guys. I think I heard something," whispered Hanny, as he stood and moved stealthily into the woods.

The boys looked around nervously, hearing rustling in the brush.

"Look out!"

A figure with a terrifying mask had leaped out of the forest, howling. The boys started screaming, looking for an escape route.

But there was nowhere to go.

And then Hanny took off the mask.

"Sorry, guys. This is an Aztec mask, one of those used in their ceremonies down in the jungle. Thought I'd do a little show and tell tonight. Anyway, I think I've told you enough about where I've been and what I've seen. What I'd like to do on this, our last night together, is ask you what you think we can all learn from the time we've spent out here. Maybe we can see if it's anything like what I learned during my time down there. Anyone? Ricky?"

"I think we learned that wasps don't like to travel. They like to stay close to home."

"How so, Ricky?"

"Well, whenever a wasp started buzzing around me, I'd shoo him away, but he'd come right back. So, I'd have to do it again, and then again. But if we were hiking and I kept moving, he'd stop after a while. I think he thought when I was in his territory, he could do what he wanted, because I was on his turf."

"Do you think other creatures are territorial as well?"

"I think so. Like my mother always telling my dad to get out of the kitchen."

The group laughed.

"Okay, but is there anything or anyplace that no one can say is his own or her own?"

"The mountains?" a boy named Billy ventured. "No one owns them. They're for all of us, I think."

Everyone was quiet for a moment.

"I think so, too, Billy. I think so, too. You know, when I was hiking through South America, I saw many temples and monuments that powerful people made others build for them," Hanny said. "I think they did it to project an image of themselves as being better than regular people, but of course that wasn't true. They were more powerful than the other people, but they weren't better than them. Sometimes, they used their power to hurt others, instead of helping them. Then time went by, and they were gone. The temples and monuments were still there, but after a while everyone forgot who had ordered their construction. Centuries passed, and the jungle grew back, the vines climbed up the sides of the structures and covered them over, and the walls started to crumble, until there really wasn't much left.

"But the jungle is still there, and so are their mountains," Hanny said. "Just like our forest and our mountains. All of this is for all of us, not just a few, and it's our job to protect it. If we build, we won't build to show off. We'll build only what we need, and then we'll build to help others, and you know what? I think you guys are going to lead the way."

Hanny stood up.

"Okay boys, that's enough for tonight. Let's clean up here and turn in. We'll be breaking camp early tomorrow morning and hiking back to Stoney House, so we can get there in time for lunch."

An hour later, he ducked into his tent. He felt good about where he was, what he had learned, and what lay in the future.

He had made the right decision.

53

THE NEXT MORNING, as the hikers broke camp, Tim was on his way to Vermont. In the region just north of New York City, the leaves on the trees had turned fully, but they lost their luster and could be seen dropping to the ground as he moved further north. By the time he turned east toward southern Vermont, the battle had been lost, and the fields were littered with casualties. Another fall foliage season was nearing its end.

How fitting, Tim thought, for the news he had to deliver. He still hadn't decided just what he would say to Hanny. What did one tell a total novice in the investment arena, when he has been battered and bloodied before even putting on the gloves? In a tragic way, it was appropriate, given what the young fellow saw as the shortcomings of societies that worshipped wealth and power. Still, he should have been permitted a calm interlude, however brief, before the forces of money crushed him underfoot.

Tim's apprehension grew as he approached the little town of Danby, which Mike Green had just recently informed him was the onetime home of Pearl Buck. Years earlier, the American author had won both the Pulitzer Prize and the Nobel Prize for her novel *The Good Earth*, about a peasant farmer's life in China. Tim had read the book some time before, but had been unaware of Buck's Vermont connection. That he had learned when Mike had noted the obvious correlation between *The Good Earth* and Hanny's fascination with the earth and nature, and, at times, the dissolution that comes when wealth intrudes.

Thinking of that now, Tim drove through the town and began the sometimes steep climb up the winding road to Danby Four Corners. Ten minutes and several hundred feet of elevation later, he turned into the Smokey House Center's parking area. Getting out of his car, he looked around at the now familiar stables, pens and fields, and started to walk toward the main building.

Then he stopped.

54

A SMALL BAND OF CAMPERS was coming out of the woods on the far side of the road. They walked toward him over a field of freshly mown hay.

It was Hanny's group.

Tim waited until they began to cross the road, and then he started in their direction, until Hanny saw him.

"Tim? I didn't know you were coming back. Is your boy with you?"

"Hi, Hanny. No, it's just me."

"It's nice to see you, but ... is something wrong? You look upset."

"Hanny, I'm sorry. Something happened while you were away."

"Is it Mom? Is she sick?"

"No, your mother is fine. It's not anything like that. Maybe we can talk privately while your hikers unwind. I'll wait if you need to speak with them first."

"All right. Just give me a minute, will you?"

"Sure. I'll wait right here."

Hanny led his charges over to the main house. He invited

them to shed their backpacks and gear, and leave everything outside. When that was done, they could go into the dining hall and get some lunch. He said he'd join them in a few minutes. Then he went back to where Tim stood, waiting for him.

"Okay, Tim. What is it? What happened?"

There was no way to break this gently.

"The market crashed on Monday."

"What market?"

"The stock market. The stock market crashed."

"What do you mean crashed?"

"There were huge losses all across the board. Everything was dropping. People panicked and started selling. The options traders got killed, especially the ones like your uncle, the ones who were heavy into call options. Then the margin calls started. Hanny, I'm sorry."

"You say this happened on Monday?"

"Yes. I couldn't reach Hal Baker on the phone, so I rushed over to his office, hoping he could do something to protect the estate account, but he wasn't there. They said he had called in sick. I knew he was going on vacation starting Tuesday, but I guess he just figured he'd get an early start on it. No one else even knew who I was. It was hopeless. We won't be able to reach him until the day after tomorrow, and, obviously, there won't be anything he can do by then."

"But Tim, Hal said everything would be finalized in three days, and that was just for trades to be, I think he called it, 'settled.' He said they were actually final on day one, but they wouldn't 'close' until the third day."

"When did he say that?"

"The week before last. You know, when you and I met with him at his office. That was one of the things he told me after you left. He also said to give him a call if I had any questions, or had made any decisions. Didn't he tell you?"

"Well, yes. I spoke to him the next day."

"You mean Wednesday?"

"Yes, Wednesday afternoon, the day after we went to see

him. He did mention that you might call, but said he hadn't heard from you yet. I assumed you'd decided to wait until you got back from this trip."

"You didn't speak to him again?"

"No. Why?"

Hanny started to smile.

"So, you didn't know that I called him Thursday afternoon?"

"No."

"Or that I told him to sell everything?"

"What? You did? And did he?"

"Yeah, he did. I called him again, on Friday morning before we started the hike, to make sure. He said it was all done."

Tim threw out his arms and grabbed Hanny in a bear hug.

"All right! All right!" Tim shouted, so loud that he startled a flock of sheep in a nearby pen, causing them to run to the furthest corner. Even the boss ram looked uncertain of whether to look threatening, or cower with the ewes.

Hanny laughed, extricated himself from the bear hug, and gave Tim a high five, but sobered somewhat as he realized the implications of the news Tim had come to share.

"Did a lot of people get hurt?"

"Yes, they did, Hanny. Many people did. I'm just glad you weren't one of them. What made you decide to sell?"

"It's hard to say. Look at what happened to my uncle. It became an obsession with him. He got caught up in this urge for more and more, forgetting everything that he had pledged to do—for his clients, for my father, for everyone. The power of money took hold of him. He was going to be taller than the rest, someone people would look up to and admire. In a sense, to idolize. He forgot that some of them might get hurt in the process.

"I knew nothing about investing, and all of a sudden I was supposed to do it myself, to make more money, even though I didn't need more. I didn't even need what was already there. Then I thought maybe I could use some of it to help others. I decided to sell everything, and just put the money in the bank, so I could do that."

"That's when you called Hal Baker?"

"No, because I started to feel guilty, thinking maybe my father had been right. He might have said I should start to act like an adult, instead of a naive idealist, an immature romantic.

"I was also afraid of how Hal Baker would react if I told him to sell everything. He might say I was just panicking. So I kept putting it off. I still hadn't called him by the time I left for Vermont that Thursday.

"Then, on the way up here, the bus driver, of all people, told me something. What he said made me realize that what I had decided to do in the first place was exactly what I should do, and so I did it. I got off the bus at a rest stop, went to a pay phone, and called Hal. I told him to sell everything, and he didn't argue. He said I was just in time, that the stock market was going to close in less than a half hour, and that he had to get off the phone right away, and 'go to work on it.'

"I called him the next day before we started out on our hike, wanting to make sure he had done it. That was a week ago yesterday."

"The last day of trading before 'Black Monday,'" Tim said.

"Yes. I guess so."

"Oh, this is fabulous, Hanny. Wait until everyone back home hears. Your mother, my wife, Connie Logan over at Surrogate's. I'm going to call Marge right now."

Tim started toward the main house, then stopped.

"But wait. You said the bus driver told you something. What was it?"

"He said that all of us are really the same, and the only reason we should reach higher is so that we can see the stars, not so everyone else can look up to us. Then I knew, because here in Vermont I can see the stars. These mountains are the temples, and we need to preserve them. Now I believe that's really what my father would have wanted me to do and he gave me what I needed to do it."

— Epilogue —

HANNY NEVER DISCOVERED the grand unified theory, but he remained intrigued by the concept of dark energy, thinking it might someday provide the answer to what lies beyond the stars. He moved to Vermont, and became a strong supporter of environmental causes—especially a charity called Vermonters for a Clean Environment, after it was founded in 1999 by Annette Smith, another famous Danby resident.

Hanny looked up Margaret again, and she agreed to meet him one day at Jay Peak. They had lunch, and she told him she had finally found "the right guy." After his initial disappointment, he realized she was talking about him. They married a year later.

He declined Tim's suggestion that he consider suing his uncle Chris for the commissions and fees he had taken improperly. Hanny said Chris needed the money more than he did and, besides, he already had enough himself.

In time, Hanny decided that keeping several million dollars in his checking account, while somewhat consistent with his belief that he had enough money already, wasn't consistent with his desire to help others with the money. Only the bank would be served by leaving the money uninvested, and the funds would lose value as inflation ate into them over the years. Given that, he bought long term U.S. Treasury bonds, which were paying nearly 9% per annum after the 1987 crash.

Tim encouraged Katie to take ballet lessons. She declined, telling her parents that she wanted to become an actress instead, having been inspired by her role in *It's a Wonderful Life*. Her performance was well received, although she created something of a stir when she got bored waiting for her cameo appearance on stage. She opened the cage housing "Uncle Billy's" crow so she could play with it. The crow escaped and flew out into the high school auditorium, to the sound of shrieking mothers and laughing siblings. The ushers finally captured the bird and returned it to its cage, there to await its next scene.

Timmy decided that Maisie lived too far away and, besides, there was a really nice girl in his school who knew how to ski.

Tim and Mike went ahead with the expansion of their office, hiring Mandy Schwartz as their second full-time secretary, and convincing Connie Logan to join them as the third partner, renaming the firm Green, O'Leary and Logan.

Tim and Marge became ardent skiers, and traveled regularly to Vermont to enjoy the slopes and renew their love affair with the state, and each other.

It took a while, but Marge succeeded in tracking down her client Mary's birth mother, Sandra, who was still alive but failing rapidly. Marge's efforts were aided by what she had learned in searching for Hanny. She checked with the trust officer responsible for Sandra's trust, and was pleased to find that Sandra had make him the designated representative for learning what borders she had crossed in her travels. The last had been Monaco, and Sandra was quickly found in that tiny principality. A reunion was arranged, and mother and daughter spent three touching weeks together before the end came. Mary felt it was unfair to claim the entire trust, so she decided that the charitable beneficiary should receive a third, with Mary getting the rest.

One day, when Marge stopped by Tim's office to review the agreement between Mary and the charity, they decided to invite Mrs. Murphy to come along on their next ski trip. It would be a good chance for her to visit Hanny in his new home. Tim called her in.

"Mrs. Murphy, my wife and I are taking a ride up to Vermont with the children next weekend. We thought you might want to come along, so you could pay a visit to Hanny and his new wife."

"Oh, how nice you two are. I'd love to. And ... Mr. O'Leary? Mrs. O'Leary? I don't mean to be disrespectful, but ... "

"Yes?"

"Mrs. O'Leary, do you remember the time you took me to lunch and told me whenever I wanted to change, I could call you by your first name?"

"Of course."

"You know, I almost feel like we're family now. If you still mean it, I'd like to call you Marge from now on, and ... and ... Mr. O'Leary ... Tim?"

Both of them laughed.

"Why, of course, Mrs. Murphy."

"And you can call me 'Madeline.'"